From Dependency to Dignity:
Individual and Social Consequences
of a Neighborhood House

From Dependency to Dignity: Individual and Social Consequences of a Neighborhood House

by
LOUIS A. ZURCHER, PH.D., AND ALVIN E. GREEN, M.S.W.,
WITH EDWARD JOHNSON AND SAMUEL PATTON

BEHAVIORAL PUBLICATIONS, INC.
New York, N.Y.

Contents

Acknowledgments

DATA and interpretations presented in this monograph are drawn in part from a broader study of a poverty intervention organization and social change. The research was supported by OEO Grant 66-9744, and the monograph prepared as a report to the Research and Demonstrations Branch, Community Action Program, Office of Economic Opportunity, Washington, D.C.

The authors gratefully acknowledge the cooperation and comments of Highland Park-Pierce neighborhood residents and of Dr. Robert Harder and Mr. Simon Martinez, formerly of the Topeka Office of Economic Opportunity. The authors deeply appreciate the helpful critiques of Dr. Gardner Murphy, Dr. James Taylor, Dr. Roy Menninger, Dr. Herbert Modlin, Dr. William Key, Mr. Richard Benson, Mr. Arthur Mandelbaum, Mr. William Lawrence, and Mrs. Susan Zurcher. Mr. Fred Hill, a research assistant and participant observer in the Highland Park-Pierce area, substantially contributed to preparation of the monograph. The authors also acknowledge the valuable research assistance of William Simons, Rosanne Barnhill, and Basil Keiser, and the secretarial support of Sherry Schiller, Geneva Vonderschmidt, Janice Boldridge, and Winnie Anderson.

Chapter 1

Introduction

Some Assumptions about the Poor

DEPENDING upon the criteria used by estimators, there are from 20 million to 70 million "poor" persons in the United States (MacDonald, 1965; Ornati, 1965; Orshansky, 1965). Social scientists have spent considerable research time attempting to describe social and psychological concomitants of poverty. Some observers have concluded that interactive networks within groups of poor persons are complex and permanent enough to reveal a change-resisting "culture of poverty" (J. Cohen, 1964; Gans, 1965; Haggstrom, 1964; Harrington, 1963; Herzog, 1966; Leighton, 1965; O. Lewis, 1961, 1966; W. B. Miller, 1965; Riessman, Cohen, & Pearl, 1964). Others choose not to emphasize a pervading culture of poverty, but rather the types and varieties of individual response to poverty (H. Lewis, 1965; S. M. Miller, 1966; Rodman, 1965). A number of researchers have isolated possible psychosocial "characteristics" of the poor, which are considered to be products of the restrictions of poverty. Among the characteristics most often mentioned are: alienation from society, others and self; anomie; present orientation; fatalism; powerlessness; isolation; suspiciousness of and antagonism toward authority and outsiders; apathy; hostility; particularism; social and personal disorganization; a preference for the informal over the formal; feelings of inferiority; dependency; passive-aggressiveness; lack of impulse control; no sense of history; low achievement motivation and level of aspiration; fragility of social relationships; negativism; paucity of social roles; role confusion; extra-punitiveness; traditionalism; anti-intellectualism; helplessness; preference for the concrete over the abstract in language and thought; preference for doing rather than thinking; feelings of marginality; sense of resignation; hesitancy to assume leadership; feelings of insecurity; feelings of meaninglessness in their lives and in the world around them; tendency toward authoritarianism; value for tangible and immediate results from their activities (Beilin, 1956; Beiser, 1965; Bell, 1957; Bernstein, 1960; Brager, 1965; J. Cohen, 1964; A. Cohen & Hodges, 1963; Deutch, 1963; Empey, 1956; Gould, 1941; Haggstrom, 1964; Herzog, 1963; Keller, 1963; Leighton, 1965; LeShan, 1952; Levinson, 1964; O. Lewis, 1959, 1961; McClosky & Schaar, 1965; W. B. Miller, 1958; Miller & Riessman, 1961; Miller, Riessman & Seagull, 1965; Mischel, 1961; Piven, 1966; Riessman, 1962, 1964, 1966; Rosen, 1956; Rosen & D'Andrade, 1959; Schneider & Lysgaard, 1953; Simpson & Miller, 1961, 1963; Sjoberg, Brymer & Farris, 1966; Spinley, 1953; Strauss, 1962; Stone, Leighton & Leighton, 1966; Wright & Hyman, 1958; Zurcher, 1967b).

Postulations about the existence of a definable culture of poverty, the modes of individual adjustment to poverty, and the psychosocial characteristics of the poor are interesting and vital, but have not been presented here primarily to stimulate debate about preferred theoretical stance. Rather for the purposes of this book the point is taken from the literature that the economic, social and psychological conditions of poverty may serve to limit severely the poor's development of individual potential, freedom of choice, and control over events normal to daily living. A sense of powerlessness in what may be perceived to be an arbitrary environment can sustain self-doubt among the poor, and afford them little strategy — probably only detachment and/or hostility — to meet autonomy needs. Chronic official dependency upon welfare institutions can provide physical sustenance, but perhaps at a psychological price that further bankrupts client self-esteem (Haggstrom, 1964). A legacy of hopelessness and anger may be passed from parent to child, along with a rigid and inadequate set of skills with which to "make out in this lousy world," and the cycle of poverty is thus perpetuated.

The neighborhoods in which the poor live often reveal their feelings of hopelessness, alienation, and isolation. Usually, the nuclear and extended family is the most trusted and functional form of social organization within a low-income neighborhood. Other forms of social organization such as churches, semi-organized gangs, or street corner cliques may exist, but these more often than not serve to perpetuate individual members' isolation from the community-at-large (Brager, 1965; Haggstrom, 1964; Beiser, 1965; O. Lewis, 1966; Piven, 1966; Stone, Leighton, & Leighton, 1966; Wittenberg, 1948). Low-income neighborhoods differ markedly from middle-class neighborhoods in physical appearance, are clearly marked by geographical and/or topographical boundaries, and are labeled generally or specifically as "slums," "ghettos," "blighted areas," etc. It would seem that residents, for geographical reasons alone, could not help but feel distant from the community-at-large. Furthermore, for what seem to them vague reasons, they may actively experience more of the community's punishment structure than its reward structure. During their lifetime, particularly if they are members of an ethnic minority, they probably have been both overtly and covertly informed that there must be something wrong with them, a damnation "proved" by the fact that they cannot get themselves out of poverty or out of "that neighborhood." If the residents' contacts with community formal organizations have been under circumstances of enforced dependency, and if enforced dependency is unacceptable, then the relationships between helpers and helped may serve further to label pejoratively low-income people, and to intensify their isolation and alienation from the community-at-large.

If it is not possible for an individual meaningfully to participate in the community-at-large, it is still possible for him meaningfully to avoid participation in the community. Feelings of rejection thus can be turned into an exertion of one's own will. Some semblance of self-esteem or self-determination can be salvaged by active detachment from a community that is psychologically and in some cases physically rejecting. "Who needs the community?" becomes an implicit motto. If detachment is not enough to abate the indignities of poverty and its associated frustrations, then more drastic and aggressive forms of behavior may be inaugurated. The implicit motto then becomes "Look what I can do to the community!"

Throughout this monograph the authors will accept two assumptions about the needs of human beings: (1) that a human being strives to maintain a degree of self-esteem with which he feels comfortable; and (2) that a human being experiences stress when he must live in an environment in which he feels powerless. Following these assumptions, the characteristics of the poor described above are seen by the authors as attempts to cope with a specific set of social and physical circumstances. Such coping behavior over time, over generations, may begin to take on the structure of a life style that can become increasingly resistant to change.

Since one of the results of a life of poverty may be a defensive and motivated withdrawal from the community as a perceived source of psychological and physical harm, it can be difficult for poor persons to allow themselves enough personal contact with community formal organizations to discover, as members of other socioeconomic classes discover, that such organizations can be *used;* one does not necessarily have to be passive when interacting with them. Thus the poor may choose to dig in on their own "turf," such as it is, and in a very real sense resist change. How does one deal with this complex problem? How does one stimulate changes in confidence, motivation and skill among the poor, and at the same time stimulate changes in societal socioeconomic structures that have been observed to create and maintain conditions for poverty? In 1964, the Economic Opportunity Act proclaimed a national strategy toward resolving that complex problem.

The Poor's War on Poverty

The Economic Opportunity Act of 1964 established the Office of Economic Opportunity, declared a "War on Poverty" and made program funds available to applicant communities throughout the United States. A primary intent of the Economic Opportunity Act was to stimulate or accelerate change in the socioeconomic structures of communities by going beyond the usual expedient of mechanically supplying material resources to the poor. The plan was to involve the poor, through "maximum feasible participation," in decisions and processes that led to resource acquisition (Economic Opportunity Act, 1964). The strategy of funds, programs and active involvement of the poor was designed with the hope of disrupting the cycle of poverty.

On paper, "maximum feasible participation" was an invitation to the poor to exert power and control in newly formed organizations that were to be concerned with their welfare. In contrast to more traditional community techniques for dealing with the poor, beneficiaries were to be among the decision-makers, "clients" were to be colleagues. A prevailing assumption of the Presidential task force that helped prepare the Economic

Opportunity Act had been that unilateral and arbitrary providing to the poor by the not-poor often served to institutionalize rather than ameliorate poverty. Since continuing dependency of the poor — official and unofficial — seemed to be a major problem, it was felt that something more had to be done to stimulate self-help among the poor and to open opportunity for their gaining a sense of dignity and belonging in society-at-large. "Maximum feasible participation," though a somewhat vaguely defined phrase, was thus at least in part intended to begin reversing the dependency process often reinforced by already existing welfare bureaucracies. Furthermore, it was hoped that significant participation in the various OEO-sponsored poverty programs would multiply social roles and skills, encourage indigenous leadership, and generate self-competence and seeking motivations among the poor.

The implementation of the concept "maximum feasible participation" in itself may engender significant social change. Jealously guarded professional status, safe distances from clients, coveted political and economic powers, and cherished stereotypes can be challenged by meaningful entry of the previously disenfranchised poor into areas of decision-making and power within the community. If successful, participation of the poor could redistribute not only goods and services within the community, but also influence and control. However, attempts toward such changes usually elicit at least some resistance from those with vested interests in the status quo.

The Neighborhood House as a Strategy

Title II of the Economic Opportunity Act enables qualifying communities to establish local coordinating agencies and subsequently to apply for specific community action programs. Among the various community action programs funded by the Office of Economic Opportunity, perhaps the most advantageous for implementing maximum feasible participation of the poor is the neighborhood house. Ideally, these vest-pocket organizations have primarily been requested, developed, and operated by neighborhood residents themselves. The house has the potential for accomplishing far-reaching goals. It can serve as a training ground for the participating poor in which they develop organizational skills, new and more complex social roles, and a sense of identity with peers, neighborhood, and the broader community. The house can stimulate a sense of ownership among participants and others in the neighborhood, allowing them significant control over and immediate results from activities of which they are the beneficiaries. The neighborhood house can provide a shift in agency-client relationships — the neighborhood residents *invite* the cooperation of community agencies through their neighborhood house. The latter establishes neighborhood residents as the instigators of agency operations, instead of (their more typical roles) passive recipients of services. At the same time the cooperating agencies can find a new access to perhaps previously unreachable persons, and thus better accomplish their organizational purposes. This access may be expanded even further by the house's providing indigenous workers who could approach the unaffiliated poor more readily and less threateningly than agency personnel (Rciff & Riessman, 1965). The neighborhood residents could orient to the neighborhood house in a fashion unlike previous experiences with organizations. They would have a hand in determining what specific poverty programs the house would undertake, based upon their perceptions of neighborhood needs, and perhaps begin to understand the utility and usability of organizations for accomplishing specific goals. The roles and attitudes developed by participation in and contact with the neighborhood house might be generalized to other community organizations, and encourage the poor to interact with the latter in a less passive and dependent fashion.

The neighborhood house further has the potential of being a locus for effective and indigenously determined social action. A number of observers have reported the striking benefits that participation in social action has had upon the self-esteem and personal adjustment of the participants. Powerlessness, dependency, alienation and apathy can fall away with the reaching of meaningful self-determined and self-attained goals (Beiser, 1965; Haggstrom, 1964; Leighton, 1965; Pearlman, 1965; Stone, Leighton & Leighton, 1966; Wittenberg, 1948). Similarly, social action revolving around meaningful issues has been demonstrated to create a sense of neighborhood where little but geographical proximity existed before (Criminger, 1965; Leighton, 1965; MacCoby, 1958). Ideally, then, the neighborhood house could have wide impact upon a low-income neighborhood, its residents, and their reciprocal interactions. The dynamics of the generative process of participation, ownership, and self-direction could generalize to resident and neighborhood association with other components of the community-at-large.

In order to acquire government funds for the establishment of a neighborhood house, or any other OEO community action program, the applicant body must provide at least 10 percent of the total cost of the program as a local share. More often than not the most ready sources for local share contributions are the already existing community agencies. Those agencies, sometimes serving as "delegate agencies" and thus assuming a degree of supervisory responsibility for the program, are inclined to consider the implementation of their standing policies more important than innovating for the participation and self-determination of the beneficiaries. Such a view can be unfortunate, and may render impossible the intent of the Economic Opportunity Act (Brager, 1965; Gans, 1965; Haggstrom, 1964). A crucial point to be made is that agency expansion of outreach and services through an OEO program is not necessarily obstructed by "maximum feasible participation" of the poor. To the contrary, their participation can facilitate agency goals.

There is no doubt that a neighborhood house needs agency cooperation and expertise. Furthermore, many of the social problems contacted by a neighborhood house have traditionally been concerns of established agencies, and the accumulation of their experiences can save the neighborhood house costly mistakes and duplications. However, unless the neighborhood house *invites* the cooperation of the agencies, the typical role distance between the not-poor helpers and the helped poor may be maintained, and nothing changes. If an agency exerts tight control over a neighborhood house it may have some opportunity to improve the quality and quantity of services to low-income people, but it probably will not provide the participative *process experience* for the poor which can subsequently engender significant psychosocial change among them.

OEO neighborhood-based programs exist under an assortment of names, some proper names, some generic. In this paper we shall use the term "neighborhood house" to refer both to a specific case and to an idea: (1) the specific organization studied and here presented; and (2) the idea of a neighborhood organization that maximizes opportunity for participation of the residents and encourages development of indigenous: (a) sense of ownership, (b) social roles, (c) self-confidence, (d) feelings of control over and power within the environment, (e) self-determination, and (f) choice of alternatives in matters concerning daily living. The neighborhood house is seen not as an isolated organization at war with the rest of the community, nor as an agency-owned affiliate. Rather, the neighborhood house is conceptualized as a bridge, perhaps temporary in nature, between alienated poor and uninterested, misinformed or uninvolved not-poor. Of prime importance, the neighborhood house is conceptualized as the property, the "turf" of the neighborhood people — and no others. As thus idealized, the neighborhood house is seen as a strategy and an agent for social change.

Research Setting and Method

Topeka, the capital city of Kansas, has a population of approximately 125,000, with 8 percent Negro, 3.5 percent Mexican-American, and 0.8 percent American Indian. Typical of many rural and smaller urban areas in the Midwest, Topeka by no means presents the image of a depressed area. There are no crowded tenements, no blocks of shanties, nor any of the other dramatic and headline-making evidences of social hurts. Nonetheless, inspection of the indices of deteriorated housing, unemployment, substandard education, and other components of economic deprivation within subdivisions of the city reveals chronic but well-behaved poverty.

In May, 1965, the national Office of Economic Opportunity approved a community action agency planning grant for Topeka, Kansas. The grant application had been submitted by the Topeka Welfare Planning Council, a group composed of middle and higher socioeconomic-class professionals and agency representatives. The community action agency subsequently was staffed and named the Topeka Office of Economic Opportunity (hereafter, the Topeka OEO).

The Topeka Welfare Planning Council, which had provided local share of funding, and the Topeka OEO staff determined that Topeka's poverty program would attempt to implement the mandates of the Economic Opportunity Act — particularly concerning participation of the poor. The planners felt that the Topeka OEO should be "on middle ground" (Topeka OEO, 1965-66, p.10), not identifying with the poor or not-poor but striving to bring together representatives from both segments toward community action and social change. (For a discussion of the dynamics of a poverty intervention organization that attempts to maintain "middle ground," see: Zurcher, 1967a.) The planners postulated that interaction of representatives from the poor with representatives from the community power structure, in programs geared for the amelioration of poverty, would serve to breakdown mutual stereotypes, enhance communication, and provide the poor with the opportunity to learn the organizational skills whereby they could acquire an active and substantial role in community affairs. (For a conceptualization of this model for social change, see: Zurcher & Key, 1967.)

To mobilize the program and to provide the machinery for planning and implementing OEO community action proposals, the Topeka OEO staff, with the advice of the Topeka Welfare Planning Council, developed three major committee components: (1) Study Committees: 11 subject-matter committees, i.e., housing, employment, education, etc., whose task was to provide low-income neighborhood people with resource data on needs and alternative solutions; (2) Target Neighborhood Committees: 12 committees, each representing a specified low-income target neighborhood, having elected officers, and whose task was to serve as a forum for neighborhood and individual needs and plans of action; and (3) The Economic Opportunity Board: intended to be the major decision-making body of the community action agency, incorporated and empowered with budgetary, personnel and program control, and composed of at most 75 voting members, including chairmen and vice-chairmen of the Target Neighborhood Committees and representatives from local agencies and civic organizations. The Study Committees and the Economic Opportunity Board both drew at least one-third of their membership from among the poor. All of the members of Target Neighborhood Committees were residents of low-income areas. (For a more detailed description of the organizational structure, see: Topeka OEO, 1965-66, pp. 57-59.) The Topeka OEO organizationally was in the employ and under the direction of the Economic Opportunity Board. It was designed to act as a coordinating body for the committee components and their representatives, to process and prepare grant applications at the direction of the committees, and to serve as liaison between the community of Topeka and Federal granting agencies.

In September, 1966, Louis A. Zurcher began a study of the

Topeka Poverty Program and its relation to some aspects of social change, research later supported by a grant from the national Office of Economic Opportunity. (At the time of writing, he was with the Menninger Foundation. He is now in the Department of Sociology, University of Texas.) Specifically, the Topeka study was concerned with the organizational dynamics of the Topeka OEO as a poverty intervention organization, the development of neighborhood action groups in the Target Neighborhood Committees, the emergence and dynamics of indigenous leadership, and members interaction and decision-making in the Economic Opportunity Board (see, e.g., Zurcher, 1966, 1967a, 1967b, 1967c; Zurcher & Key, 1967). In order to minimize interference with social action endeavors of the poverty program and to maximize rapport with the participants, the research mainly utilized the field techniques of participant observation and unstructured interviews. Parallel observers and follow-up interviews were used wherever and whenever possible in order to strengthen the reliability of the data. Up to June, 1967, over 200 committee meetings had been attended and documented, and daily contact had been maintained with Topeka OEO staff and participating representatives from the poor and not-poor.

One of the Target Neighborhood Committees, Highland Park-Pierce, acquired Federal funds to establish a neighborhood house in their area. The establishment, maintenance, and dynamics of the neighborhood house are to be described below. As part of the larger study of the Topeka poverty program, participant observers attended all Highland Park-Pierce Target Neighborhood Committee, Study Committee, and Economic Opportunity Board meetings that dealt with the proposal for and implementation of the neighborhood house. Activities of the Topeka OEO staff important to the neighborhood house were also recorded. Alvin E. Green, a social worker, was accepted by the neighborhood house as their consultant from an agency providing the local share of funding. From May, 1966, until this writing in September, 1967, he worked approximately

15 hours a week in close association with the staff of the neighborhood house, the principal participants in its development, and with many residents of the Highland Park-Pierce area. As part of his work, he daily recorded his observations of neighborhood and house dynamics. Edward Johnson was the first and still is director of the Highland Park-Pierce Neighborhood House, and recorded many of his observations as a central participant from February, 1966, until this writing. Samuel Patton has been chairman of the Highland Park-Pierce Target Neighborhood Committee since its beginning in June, 1965, was instrumental in the activities that led to and now sustain the neighborhood house, and has maintained close contact with the research staff. The multiple authorship of this monograph provides, therefore, an integration of both research and action purviews of significant events contributing to the case history of the Highland Park-Pierce Neighborhood House.

This exploratory study will report some aspects of the growth and development of a neighborhood house as a social intervention organization. The focus of the study was upon those individuals who actively participated in the planning, implementation, operation, direction and activities of the house. Some of the experiences of the approximately 500 low-income active participants are presented, particularly as they relate to observed personal and social change in the neighborhood and in the community-at-large.

The Highland Park-Pierce Neighborhood

An area of about 400 acres near the southeast corner of Topeka was designated by the Topeka OEO as the Highland Park-Pierce Target Neighborhood. The area is rectangular in shape and bisected by working tracks of the Santa Fe Railroad. Four major thoroughfares constitute its boundaries, on the other side of which begin light industries, businesses, and middle-class residential districts.

Earlier in Topeka's history, the area designated as the Highland Park-Pierce Neighborhood was on the edge of the city of Topeka, and on the "wrong side of the tracks." In 1950 the township of Highland Park, population 7,000, was annexed to the city, and with it the rectangular parcel of "no man's land" between it and the city. That parcel, the Highland Park-Pierce Target Neighborhood, did not develop at the same pace as other areas across its borders.

Census data from 1965 and current neighborhood surveys reveal the Highland Park-Pierce Target Neighborhood to be suffering economically, virtually an island within the larger community. Eighty percent of the roads in Highland Park-Pierce are unpaved; over half of the homes are more than 25 years old and are shack-like in appearance. Highland Park-Pierce has the highest incidence of inadequate plumbing facilities and the highest incidence of housing "blight" in the city of Topeka. The average property value in Highland Park-Pierce is $5,500 compared with a city average of $12,500. The topography, as one observer commented,

> . . .resembles the old photographs of Topeka when board shacks dotted the prairie. Now, hard dirt roads, pocked by chuckholes and hard chunks of buried rock, favor horse-drawn vehicles rather than automobiles. During the summertime giant stalks of weeds — some 10 feet high — choke the vacant lots, infest the open areas and grow in the ditches along the road, obscuring one neighbor's shack from another. In the winter, the leafless skeletons of thickets and hedge apple trees and the gray bleakness of the shacks make it hard to believe that you are in the midst of a community of 120,000 people. Ironically, one can stand at night on the high ground in Highland Park-Pierce and see the lights from the big shopping complexes to the south and north blaze all around the lonely darkness. Except for a trickle of commuters taking shortcuts through the area, Highland Park-Pierce might just as well be located in the middle of a prairie.

Other manifestations of chronic poverty are revealed in this neighborhood, which is 85 percent Negro, 15 percent Anglo-Saxon, and has a total population of approximately 1,200. Nearly

30 percent of the families have an income of $3,000 or less; another 30 percent an income of $5,000 or less. The average length of school attendance for children in Highland Park-Pierce is 9.5 years, compared with a Topeka average of 12.1 years. Highland Park-Pierce has the highest unemployment rate, 9.3 percent, in the city, is second highest in juvenile offenses, second highest in illegitimate births, and highest in per capita rate of venereal disease.

The residents in the Highland Park-Pierce Target Neighborhood apparently have felt little identification with their own neighborhood or with the community-at-large. One of the indigenous leaders in the area summarized the views of the residents with whom he had discussed that matter.

> They just don't feel that they are in the mainstream of the society here. Sometimes we get the feeling that we're almost living in another country. Now it's not that we have poverty like they have in the big cities where everyone is jammed all together. We don't have that. But in some ways what we have is worse. That's because nobody notices us. There are no big streets that come through Highland Park-Pierce so other people can see that there really is poverty here. This area is kind of like a whirlpool, you know, where all kinds of cars and people go running around the outside, but they never see the deep hole in the middle. Lots of us have jobs in other parts of the city, but all our other activities are right here in Highland Park-Pierce. Our kids usually play here too, although there are almost no organized things for them to do. What breaks my heart is that we've got so much potential here. Did you know that only about 70 acres out of this whole area have houses on them that are in use? Look at all that land that we could develop if we knew how, or if we could get somebody to show us how. Well, I don't know how we're going to do it. But somehow we've got to get attention to ourselves. Those people in Watts got attention to themselves. I don't like that way, and I hope we never have to do it that way. I hope we can maybe find some other way first.

Chapter 2

The Highland Park-Pierce
Neighborhood Committee

T HE Highland Park-Pierce Neighborhood Committee held
its first meeting in the social room of a neighborhood
church on an evening early in July, 1965. The first and the
following meetings were organized and primarily conducted by
the assistant director of the Topeka OEO, as he carried out
his commission to develop Target Neighborhood Committees
and to inform neighborhood residents about the structure,
function, and potential of the poverty program. The modal group
dynamics of the early meetings, held twice monthly and attended
by an average of 20 members each, were: general orientation,
catharsis of personal and group grievances, emergence of
indigenous leadership, and gradual focus upon specific needs
and plans of action (Zurcher, 1967c). By the end of July, the
Neighborhood Committee had elected a chairman, vice-chairman, and secretary and had moved their meeting place to a
shelter house in the neighborhood's small park. All three of
the committee's elected officers and all of the participating

committee members were Negro. Approximately half of the attending members were female, and the age range for the total membership extended from teenagers through senior citizens. All but a few of the participants were "poor" by the OEO financial criteria.

Each meeting was opened with a prayer offered by a chairman-designated member. A sample of the prayer, which usually followed the same theme, is:

> Dear God, thanks for the opportunity to get together tonight, and we pray for peace and harmony here so that we can help ourselves and help others who don't have what we do. Help us to learn about all these programs and how to use them the way they will do some good. Help us to find the answers to poverty and ways to get more dignity for ourselves and the rest of our people.

As the meetings progressed, the assistant director of the Topeka OEO phased out as an active organizer, and indigenous leadership took hold of the Neighborhood Committee meetings. The assistant director continued attending the meetings, but in a consultant capacity — speaking only when questioned by officers or members.

A First Proposal

Shortly after the election of their officers, the Neighborhood Committee members began working toward sponsorship of an OEO Community Action Proposal. The members' early discussion primarily focused on needs for recreation within the neighborhood. Consideration of these problems yielded to consideration of the problems of neighborhood youths in general, and next to a broader consideration of the general isolation of the neighborhood population from knowledge about and utilization of available community services. Dialogue among members of the Highland Park-Pierce Neighborhood Committee, members of various Study Committees, representatives of the Topeka Recreation Commission, and the Topeka OEO staff resulted in a consensus on the need for an Extension Worker

Program. The extension workers would be hired from various target neighborhoods in the community and would serve as ombudsmen between neighborhood residents and community agencies or service organizations. The Recreation Commission agreed to be the delegate agency and to contribute the mandatory 10 percent local share of overall program funding. The Highland Park-Pierce Neighborhood Committee agreed to be one of the proposal sponsors.

Members of the Highland Park-Pierce Committee diligently conducted surveys and gathered letters of support required for an OEO action proposal. The interactions stimulated during the proposal preparation seemed gratifying to all the participants. The not-poor, approached for advice and support, were surprised and educated by the dedication and ability of the participating poor. The target neighborhood residents were surprised and encouraged by the cooperation of the not-poor. The Topeka OEO planners were pleased that the mixing of representatives from different socioeconomic levels in the pursuit of the community action proposal seemed to be having the intended effect: breaking down stereotypes, enhancing communication, and developing new skills.

By mid-August, after having been processed through the Topeka OEO Committee review structure, the extension worker community action proposal was enthusiastically forwarded to Washington through the regional Office of Economic Opportunity.

"We Blew It"

Over four months elapsed before Highland Park-Pierce Neighborhood Committee members learned that the extension worker proposal had been approved by the Office of Economic Opportunity in Washington. During the interim, several changes were made in the proposal at the suggestion of regional OEO and the local delegate agency—changes made to accommodate the proposal to standing or recently established organizational policies and guidelines. Committee members began to perceive the extension worker proposal as becoming more and more distant from them. Attendance at meetings gradually declined. In fact, the chairman canceled several meetings because he feared "the members would ask about the proposal, and I had no answers for them." During earlier meetings in which they had discussed the preparation of the application, and during those times when they had actively solicited supporting documents and agency cooperation, the members had referred to the extension worker planning as *"our* proposal." As application review wore on and as changes in the proposal were made, in the members' view somewhat arbitrarily and beyond their control, they began to refer to *"that* proposal." Finally, by late December when the Topeka OEO staff announced the proposal's approval and the delegate agency had begun implementing the program, the reference became *"their* proposal." The members apparently had lost their feeling of ownership of the proposal they had so excitedly helped to develop and submit.

In January, 1966, as the Extension Worker Program was implemented by the delegate agency, Neighborhood Committee members expressed further specific disappointments. They had expected that they would have more "say" in the launching of the program—particularly with regard to writing job descriptions and hiring personnel from among the target neighborhoods. They also had expected that the extension workers would help target neighborhood officers organize their neighborhoods and increase attendance at their meetings. The delegate agency, on the other hand, expected that the Extension Worker Program was to be its administrative and fiscal responsibility, and desired to fit that program into its superordinate organizational goals. This conflict in expectations was generated at least in part by the vagueness of the terms "maximum feasible participation" of the poor and of "delegate agency"—concepts that the neophyte Topeka OEO was not yet able clearly to define. As a result the participants, poor and not-poor, who were involved in preparing and implementing the Extension Worker Program came to their own conclusions about and created their own definitions of the issues of program power, control, and purpose. Those conclusions and definitions often conflicted operationally.

Neighborhood Committee members attempted to register complaints concerning their frustrated expectations to the Topeka OEO staff and at meetings of the Topeka Economic Opportunity Board. However, they were unable at that time to gain realization of their expectations.

At their first meeting following the approval and implementation of the Extension Worker Program, Highland Park-Pierce Neighborhood Committee members reflected upon the outcome of the proposal they had sponsored. They felt their own participation in the preparation of the proposal had been good experience and had taught them how to "talk the agency language" and to see that

> not all the agencies and agency people are alike. Some know what's happening and are willing to help us like we want to be helped; some don't know what's happening and can only help us in ways that tie us up.

Many of the members were angry because they had "lost the Extension Worker Program." A few announced that they had "had enough of this OEO" and would "never return to another meeting." Most of the members, though angry and disappointed, felt that they "just hadn't had enough experience to know any better" and had "let our say in the program get away from us." At the end of their discussion, the chairman summarized member consensus.

> Maybe this has been in a way good for us. For all of us this was the first time trying to put together something like this. The delegate agency, and other agencies like it, have done this a thousand times. They know their way around. We don't yet. Let's face it; we blew it! But I think we learned some of the ropes, and I don't think it will happen again. We are not going to quit. But we are not going to work hard on a program and then give it away again, either.

"This Time, We Know Better"

The members of the Highland Park-Pierce Committee reviewed neighborhood and individual needs revealed by the survey they had conducted while preparing the extension worker proposal. They discussed possible alternative programs with Topeka OEO staff and decided that those needs could best be met by establishing a neighborhood house in Highland Park-Pierce. The officers and representatives of the Neighborhood Committee met with study committees and Topeka OEO staff, and agreed upon the following formal goals for the proposed neighborhood house:

1. to provide a point of contact between low-income persons and existing services and to provide bridges between the persons and the services;
2. to provide a rallying point and a home base for the people of the neighborhood for the promotion of OEO and other related groups;
3. to provide a full range of counseling services for all age groups of the neighborhood;
4. to provide a place for family education in food marketing and preparation, clothing, consumer education, and any other courses which would help to strengthen family life;
5. to provide a place for part-time care of preschool children;
6. to provide an outlet for leisure-time activities for the people of the neighborhood;
7. to provide a place for the training of professionals and non-professionals in how to work with people in a low-income neighborhood (Topeka OEO, 1965-66, pp. 16-17).

For target neighborhood residents there was another major, though unwritten, purpose for the neighborhood house — "to give us the opportunity to run our own program." The latter goal was openly stated by the officers of the Neighborhood Committee, and was quite apparent in their subsequent participation in the preparation of the neighborhood house proposal.

The committee chairman carefully and consistently remained in a decision-making position through each step of the planning. The Topeka OEO staff and Study Committee representatives clearly were established and maintained in a consultative position by the officers and members of the Neighborhood Committee.

The Topeka OEO staff, aware of committee members' disappointment with their lack of participation in the implementation of the Extension Worker Program, were sympathetic to the committee's attempts to guarantee "say." However, the Topeka OEO director had, over the months he held the position, evolved a view of what constituted organizational integrity. He had worked diligently to build what he considered to be a coordinated and compact community action agency, and had not yet considered the eventuality of decentralization. As the Highland Park-Pierce Committee developed ideas for the neighborhood house, the Topeka OEO director expressed concern that the committee "might be moving too fast, and might get into trouble." The Neighborhood Committee had not yet fully defined all of the operating specifics of "say" and where it would take them. At that point in the dialogue, the neighborhood house endeavor could have failed—the Topeka OEO rigidly forcing domination and/or the Neighborhood Committee declaring premature and undefined independence. However, the relationship between the Topeka OEO and the committee did not disintegrate. Rather, the principals, not always without strain, satisfactorily hammered out new role relationships and redistributed supervisory responsibilities. This functional interaction seemed to be possible because: (1) the Topeka OEO staff and committee members had prior personal knowledge and trust in one another; and (2) the committee knew the Topeka OEO could help accomplish house goals, and the Topeka OEO staff knew the house could help accomplish Topeka OEO goals. Thus, despite strains of give and take concerning program power, both Topeka OEO staff and the Neighborhood Committee remained open to each other's opinions and were willing to compromise.

The Neighborhood Committee and the Topeka OEO staff agreed that the neighborhood house program should not be handled by a single delegate agency. Rather, the local share of funding was to be supplied, if possible, by nonrestricting organizations, and the Economic Opportunity Board would be the overall sponsor — with immediate guidance to be provided by an Advisory Council. The Advisory Council was to consist of eight neighborhood residents and seven representatives from community agencies. The Neighborhood Committee members insisted that they choose the community agency representatives who were to serve on the Advisory Council. They chose those individuals by criteria of demonstrated interests rather than organizational position. Furthermore, the Neighborhood Committee cautiously decided, with constant reference to the importance of "our continuing to have the say," which community organizations they would approach to help them accumulate local financial share. On the basis of their concern for potential house autonomy, the Neighborhood Committee requested and received most of their required local share from the Menninger Foundation. The balance of support was contributed by the Shawnee County Cooperative Extension Service — an agency which had for three months before made available, on an unconditional and invitational basis, home-making, landscaping, cooking, sewing, and Youth Club advice to the residents of the Highland Park-Pierce Neighborhood. Letters of cognizance and promise of future program cooperation were requested from and supplied by: the Juvenile Court, the County Health Department, County Welfare, the YMCA and YWCA, and the local Board of Education.

The Neighborhood Committee officers closely followed the proposal through the Topeka OEO application review procedure, and presented the case for approval to the Economic Opportunity Board. The board unanimously agreed to endorse the proposal. The chairman of the Highland Park-Pierce Neighborhood Committee, along with Topeka OEO staff, communicated the completed proposal to the regional Office of Economic Opportunity in Kansas City. After two months regional review, during all of which time the committee chairman sustained contact with regional and Topeka OEO staff, the neighborhood house proposal was approved and funded. The chairman announced the good news to committee members and, after sharing their exuberance, solemnly stated:

> Okay, we can be happy about this. But let's not get too excited, yet. Remember what happened last time. The real work is before us now. We've got to get the Neighborhood House going, the way we want to get it going! We made some mistakes with that Extension Worker program before, and it ended up not being our program anymore. This time, we know better.

> Now, who is going to be on the Leasing Committee. . .

Chapter 3

The Highland Park-Pierce
Neighborhood House

A FTER considerable exploring and a few disappointments, the Advisory Council located a building and property that they agreed were both within the budget and an appropriate setting for the development of the neighborhood house. The building, situated on a corner lot with considerable yard space, was a relatively new two-bedroom, full basement, family residence. The property was centrally located in the Highland Park-Pierce neighborhood, and the building, constructed on a small knoll, was quite visible and accessible. Neighborhood residents, particularly those on the Advisory Council, were enthusiastic about the selection. Many of them excitedly discussed what classes would be held in what rooms, how the kitchen should be set up for homemaking activities, how the basement could be fixed for a recreation room, etc. The acquisition of a tangible structure served to convince neighborhood residents who had previously been somewhat skeptical that "maybe something could be done." One resident, thumping his hand against a wall of the house, mused, "I've heard lots about all that poverty money. But this is the first time I have ever seen it do anything real." Several neighborhood residents had observed with curiosity the Advisory Council's inspection of the building before they had made the final choice. After the lease had been signed, a not-poor member of the Advisory Council asked if "we ought to get the word to the neighborhood residents right away?" A Neighborhood Committee officer laughed, and replied, "The word has been getting around; people knew all about it before the ink was dry. You can bet on that."

Hiring the Staff

Three staff members were to be hired for the neighborhood house: a director, a neighborhood aide, and a secretary. As outlined in the neighborhood house proposal, the director was to have the following qualifications: (1) a high school education plus experience; (2) a willingness to participate in a continuous education in on-the-job training to improve his skills in carrying out the project; (3) residence in a low-income neighborhood; (4) a general familiarity with social agencies in Topeka; (5) experience with working in group situations; (6) mature judgment and a sensitivity to people; (7) administrative abilities; (8) a minimum age of 25.

The neighborhood aide was to have the following qualifications: (1) at least a ninth-grade education; (2) residence in a low-income neighborhood; (3) mature judgment and a sensitivity to people; (4) a minimum of 18 years of age, age 21 desirable (Topeka OEO, 1965-66, p. 20).

The Advisory Council was to accept applications, interview candidates and make recommendations to the Economic Opportunity Board for final approval. Candidates' "person orientation" was to be a key criterion.

The Advisory Council conducted its personnel search and selection in accordance with the qualifications specified in the proposal, with one exception—they agreed that, if possible, all staff members would be hired not from a low-income neighborhood, but from the Highland Park-Pierce neighborhood itself.

From among several candidates, the Advisory Council chose a 40-year-old Negro male resident of the Highland Park-Pierce neighborhood. A married man with nine children, he had been a charter member of the Neighborhood Committee, and was employed as one of the workers in the Extension Worker Program. The director-elect helped the Advisory Council choose a Negro woman as the neighborhood aide and a Mexican-American woman as the secretary. Both women were neighborhood residents.

Here was another point in the development of the neighborhood house where rapport between the house director and the Topeka OEO director could have been disrupted. The two men differed in their preference for secretarial candidates. The issue of "who's running this show" might have become critical, had there not been a basis of trust and respect between directors. As it turned out, they argued, reasoned, and then concurred on a mutually satisfactory choice for secretary. The house director wanted a candidate who he felt was best suited "to understand the people." The OEO director was primarily impressed with a candidate's "efficiency as a secretary." After their discussions, both men admitted the value of the other's frame of reference, and a candidate was selected who manifested both the characteristics of empathy and efficiency. The selection of all three staff members, and the selection of the site for the neighborhood house, was unanimously approved at a subsequent meeting of the Economic Opportunity Board.

As an extension worker for six months, the new director of the Highland Park-Pierce Neighborhood House had accumulated considerable experience attempting to be a bridge between existing community agencies and their target populations. The low-income areas assigned to him by the delegate agency

included Highland Park-Pierce. His hiring by the delegate
agency had been applauded by neighborhood residents, as was
his performance on the job, even though they had continued to
feel frustrated with their participation in the implementation
of the Extension Worker Program. However, the new house
director had not been satisfied with his job as an extension
worker. He stated that he didn't reject

> the whole Extension Worker program. There are some parts of it that were
> good, especially those parts which gave us elbowroom to bring agency
> services to people who needed them, but who wouldn't try and get them,
> or who don't know anything about them at all. . .The part that bothered
> me most was that the decisions for the program were being made by people
> in offices with lots of experience, and the people in the neighborhoods
> with no experience weren't getting a chance to get some, the way the program
> was supposed to work. We had to bend the needs of the people to fit the
> policies of the delegate agency. The delegate agency wasn't able to bend
> its policies to fit what the people wanted in this case. I'm not sure how to
> go about getting the Neighborhood House going. But one thing for sure.
> It is going to start with the people, and go from there, if it's going to go at all.

The neighborhood house staff and members of the Advisory
Council met frequently to determine expenditures for furnishing
and stocking the house. Lists were made for things needed:
utensils, tables and chairs, cooking equipment, hardware, books,
recreational equipment, musical instruments, office equipment,
etc. Some of those items were budgeted in funds awarded by the
Office of Economic Opportunity. Other items, suggested one
of the not-poor members of the Advisory Council, "could be
donated from individuals or groups in the Community." The
resident members of the Advisory Council expressed preference
for acquiring donated materials from within the neighborhood
itself, so "the people will feel even more that the house belongs
to them, and it won't be like getting charity."

Occasionally during the first few Advisory Council meetings
the not-poor members, long experienced in organizing agency
and/or volunteer programs, found themselves dominating the
discussion. However, the fact that specific not-poor members
had been invited by neighborhood residents created a climate

of give and take in which unintended domination did not last long. A neighborhood resident member explained.

> There were some times in our early meetings where the others wanted to walk when we wanted to run and we wanted to walk when they wanted to run. But we all knew we wanted to go in the same direction, and had the same goals for the House. Sometimes we all did a lot of talking about not much important. But it didn't take us very long before we broke what was left of the sound barrier between us.

Open House

Three months after the proposal had been approved, the neighborhood house was, in the opinion of the staff, ready for a formal open house. Committees of neighborhood residents had, on weekends and during off hours, scrubbed, painted, and remodeled parts of the house to meet their needs and specifications. Some of the women had sewn and hung brightly colored curtains on the windows. A group of teenagers had cleaned and painted the basement. The kitchen was furnished with stove and refrigerator, and stocked with supplies and utensils. The main room of the house served as a reception area, and had desks for the secretary and the neighborhood aide. Its walls were decked with announcements and circulars of neighborhood activities and opportunities. One of the bedrooms was set up, with desk and files, as the director's office. The second bedroom, considered to be the most important room in the house, was the meeting room. The meeting room contained comfortable chairs and a coffee table with several large ashtrays. It was in this room that the director or any of his staff members would meet with neighborhood residents who "wanted to talk things over." The director felt that a relaxed, unofficial atmosphere was the only way that many of the neighborhood residents would willingly and easily talk about their needs and problems. "In this room," commented the director, "people can ask for help without having to trade in their dignity." He added, "There is no desk in this room, as you can see. That's because desks are the same as fences to people who aren't used to them."

Announcements of the forthcoming open house were placed in the Topeka newspapers and distributed as circulars to the neighborhood residents. Special invitations had been issued to agency and local government officials. At an earlier planning meeting, one of the neighborhood residents had expressed some concern about "who was going to be the speakers at the open house." The director smiled, and with amusement replied, "Sometimes we may have trouble getting jobs or getting respect, but we never have any trouble getting speakers."

On the morning of October 16, 1966, the staff, the Advisory Council and approximately 20 neighborhood resident volunteers pinned on identification tags, arranged the neighborhood house pamphlets that had been prepared, and put last minute touches on decorations and refreshments. A little later in the morning, when the official proceedings were about to begin, the group had increased to about 50 people, not including newspaper reporters and television cameramen. Several telegrams of congratulations had arrived from state and local officials, and a number of local dignitaries had made an appearance. Brief speeches were given by the chairman of the Neighborhood Committee, the director of the house, two city commissioners, the director of the Topeka OEO, and the then acting president of the Menninger Foundation. After the speeches, the principals gathered around a green ribbon that was scotch-taped across the entrance door of the house. Together, amid the flash of cameras, they cut the green ribbon with a pair of elementary school scissors. All those present warmly applauded, and there was much sharing of congratulations.

Throughout the rest of the day, neighborhood residents conducted tours of the house, dispensed refreshments, and shared their enthusiasm with visitors. By the end of the open house, nearly 100 people had signed the guest book, and it was estimated that a total of approximately 200 people had stopped by. That evening, newspapers and television reported the formal opening of the Highland Park-Pierce Neighborhood House.

Throughout the day neighborhood residents displayed obvious pride in and a keen sense of ownership of the neighborhood house. The members of the Advisory Council who did not live in the target neighborhood had, by agreement, played a relatively minor role in showing the house. The neighborhood people felt that this was "Highland Park-Pierce's House; residents should do the showing." The numerous references throughout the day to "our" and "we" attested to the depth of involvement of those residents who were sharing their pride with the visitors.

After all the visitors had left, and the neighborhood house had been cleaned up, the staff and a few volunteers warmly reflected the day's success. The director nodded and then said, in a tired voice, "So much for the window dressing. Now the job really begins."

Making Contacts and Building Programs

The early phase of neighborhood house operation reflected the director's extension worker experience and the general goals for the house as stated in the Annual Report of the Topeka OEO (above, page 21). The neighborhood house staff was, at this time, primarily content- rather than process-oriented. They were dedicated to facilitate for needy neighborhood residents those community services that were presently available. The staff viewed the neighborhood house as a bridge between community organizations and neighborhood residents. The staff view of the functions of the neighborhood house coincided with the views held by the clients who came to the neighborhood house for help of one kind or another. The first question asked by most of the neighborhood residents who come into contact with the house was, "What can it do *for* me?"

Three months after the house had formally opened its doors, the staff was averaging approximately 200 contacts with neighborhood residents each month, including follow-up consultation. Individual problems confronted and solved were concerned with such life basics as: housing, food and clothing, mental and physical health, employment, bail bonds and legal help, loans and financing, education, family difficulties, and recreation. Working relationships had been established with more than 20 community agencies and service organizations, including: County Welfare, Public Health Service, School Board, Family Service and Guidance, Cooperative Extension Service, YMCA, YWCA, Topeka State Hospital, The Menninger Foundation, Kansas Neurological Institute, Police Department, Juvenile and Probate Courts, Employment Service, Labor Department, City and County Commissioners, Urban Renewal, Kansas Teachers Association, Washburn University, City Library, local hospitals, Human Relations Commission, Small Business Loan Association, State Technical Assistance Office, United Fund, and local church groups. Those organizations were readily available, through the expediting of the neighborhood house staff, to residents for services, consultation, and in many cases employment opportunities. Through the operation of the neighborhood house, residents were now able to acquire services that they may not have known existed, and were able to approach organizations with whose application procedures thay may previously have been either unfamiliar or uncomfortable. Similarly, the agencies and organizations, through the efforts of the neighborhood house, gained access to an audience that had been and probably would have continued to be unavailable to them. Local government, education, public housing, employment, urban renewal, human relations commissions, and library officials, among others, specifically and formally commented on the increased quantity and quality of contacts initiated by Highland Park-Pierce residents.

But something more was being offered by the house than a proliferation of available services. That something more seemed to be apparent to many of the beneficiaries who lived in the neighborhood. They felt, for the first time, that they were initiating their contact with service organizations, and therefore felt less embarrassed about asking for help. They were able to approach relatively impersonal agencies with the personal support of the neighborhood house staff. Consequently, the agencies began to be perceived as less fearsome and formidable.

The house staff attempted to provide unquestioning and unconditional, but realistic, support to neighborhood residents. Often a staff member would accompany an individual on his first or on a difficult visit to a service organization. As a result, many neighborhood residents "learned their way around" complex organizations, and began to see them, as do members of middle and higher socioeconomic classes, as usable societal components. Thus, some neighborhood residents began to feel that the system was less constricting than their previous experience had led them to believe. They saw that, once one knew the language and "which buttons to push," there was room for negotiation within the system. A neighborhood resident summarized, "There is a lot more freedom around than I thought there was. I found that out as I learned the ropes." Successful experience in one encounter with a complex organization tended to generate self-confidence that generalized to other encounters with such organizations. For example, neighborhood house staff were contacted by a resident who had received notification from a finance company that, since his payments were in arrears, his automobile was about to be repossessed. The man unavoidably had been unable to maintain his payments as scheduled, and needed the car in order to continue his employment. However, he was certain that he had "had it," and there was nothing he could do to keep his car. He said that he had called the neighborhood house "as a last resort." The man thought he should personally contact the finance company, but stated he was "afraid to talk to them. They can talk rings around me. Besides, I haven't got a chance." The neighborhood house director met with the man, and discussed the nature of contracts, financial terms, refinancing possibilities, and interest rates, etc. The resident was surprised that "this stuff is not as bad as I thought." Armed with new information and alternatives, and supported by a phone call to the company from the house director, the resident confronted the finance company officials and satisfactorily resolved the issue. Later, he happily reported to the director he had "straightened the matter out." He added, "When I was in there talking those words and the finance people were listening to me, I was surprised that it was really me talking!"

Residents increasingly had an opportunity to perceive that they had invited service organizations into the neighborhood. This perception increased agency acceptability within the neighborhood, and increased the usability of their services. For example, one community organization, before the house had been established, had attempted to recruit resident attendance at a nutrition and cooking class. The organization representative knew there was considerable eagerness among the residents to add to their homemaking skills, but nonetheless was unable to encourage attendance. Subsequently, the house staff learned about that attempt and the neighborhood aide was assigned to meet with fellow residents who were known to be interested in nutrition and cooking. At first, informal individual chats were initiated. Those eventually led to gatherings of about 20 women, who would convene over coffee, discuss what their needs were, and how they would like to see them met. A few recipes were exchanged, and some of the ladies decided that each week they would take turns hosting the informal group and preparing the snack. As the group evolved and developed, it formulated its own interests and, with the neighborhood aide serving as a resource person, leadership emerged from among the group. After a few meetings, the women realized that their own sources of information were being exhausted. They discussed the possibility of looking outside the group for new information and counsel. Finally, they decided to invite the agency representative, whose program had failed earlier, to be a participant in the class. She agreed, and with her expert advice the group, up to this writing, continues to thrive with striking member satisfaction. The class curriculum now is no different from that of the instructor's first attempt to recruit neighborhood attendance, but there is an essential difference. The first time the agency representative had invited neighborhood residents to attend *her* formally organized class—a class which the residents had no hand in preparing or formulating. This time, however, the residents had evolved, from informal discussion, their own class and were inviting the agency representative, whose help they had decided they needed, to attend *their* gathering.

The staff of the neighborhood house was particularly concerned with the relatively high unemployment and underemployment rate in the neighborhood. However, they wanted to do more than "just get any jobs" for those in need of them. From his own experiences and from consultation with neighborhood residents, the director concluded that some unemployed men had not taken available jobs because the work was degrading, the conditions under which they had to accept employment were distasteful. "A man is not going to take a job," he commented, "if it makes him less of a man." The director shared with his staff what he thought was an important distinction—the distinction between "giving" a person a job, and his "taking" a job.

A man *takes* a job when he thinks it's worth something, not just financially. He *takes* a job when he can be proud of it, and when he can be glad to say that it belongs to him. When a man is *given* a job, he belongs to the job: the job doesn't belong to him. He also belongs to the people who give it to him, and he is expected to be grateful for something that he probably really didn't want.

The house staff were committed to find jobs for residents that were worth taking. Jobs that had no future, that did not pay a living wage, or that were undignifying to the individual were discouraged or avoided. The staff established a list of residents who were unemployed, underemployed, or who were dissatisfied with their present employment. Any time the staff came in contact with worthwhile jobs, they would distribute the information to those on their list. Opportunities for better jobs, or training that would make possible better jobs, were communicated on a neighborhood-wide basis. At this writing, the house staff had been instrumental in helping over 200 low-income persons get and hold jobs or improve their employment. Forty-five of those persons were Highland Park-Pierce residents, and approximately 30 percent had been considered to be "chronically unemployable."

The house staff had considerable success stimulating chronically unemployable residents to take and hold worthwhile jobs. One of the reasons for their success was that they chose to ignore the unfavorable work histories that prevented some individuals from getting any but demeaning work. The effectiveness of the staff's treating a man with unemployment problems like any other human being is perhaps best demonstrated by the following example. A 25-year-old resident with a long history of employment transiency and drinking came to the neighborhood house in search of "any job that will pay a few bucks." His frankly stated reason for wanting a job was to earn enough money to buy a full bottle. He didn't specify the kind of work he wanted, because he was convinced that he would, as always, "end up carrying the slop anyway." The house staff wouldn't go along with his view of himself; they told him they thought he was selling himself short. Working his way through stages of negativism, confusion, and sarcastic humor, the man finally agreed to accept what the house staff offered straightforwardly as a challenge. The director and the applicant together found an employment situation that offered the best opportunity and highest wages the applicant had ever experienced. The employer, the director, and the applicant openly discussed his potentials and limitations, and all agreed that he should not be hindered by his past record. The man was hired, and for four and one-half months maintained steady and successful employment — the longest period of time he had remained on any job in his working life. However, the holiday season was approaching, and the man was afraid he was going to succumb to temptation. He stated that he liked his job, and "didn't want to foul up." Having on a number of occasions shared with the house director his pride in himself for "making it on the job," he went to the director with his dilemma. He felt he couldn't get by the Christmas holidays without "hitting the bottle"; it had been a habit pattern for too many years of his short life. Yet he did not want to give up what he had finally gained. Once again, director, employer, and employee got together and honestly confronted his problem. On the strength of his record on the job, the employer agreed to grant him a two-week leave of absence without pay during the Christmas holidays. Promptly at 8:30 on the morning when his leave of absence had elapsed, the employee, after two rousing weeks, returned to the job. "Man," he confided to the director, "it didn't seem to be as much fun anymore. I'm glad to be back." He has been steadily and satisfactorily on the job since that time. For this man, the neighborhood house had provided a friendly ground upon which the burdens of his past could, at his own pace and by his own choosing, be shed with dignity for a more productive future.

While making contacts, building programs, and providing services with the added purpose of enhancing the dignity of neighborhood residents, the house staff were firmly establishing themselves, and the whole concept of a neighborhood house, as worthy of trust. No price, material or psychological, was expected for help from the neighborhood house. Assistance was intended to conform to the individual, not vice versa. The house was on neighborhood "turf," and staffed by "our own people." Support, in whatever form wanted, was there whenever and however wanted. No restrictions, no criticism, implicit or explicit, were associated with assistance—unless the individual "tried to sell himself short." The increasing trust in and realization of the usefulness of the neighborhood house is reflected in its increasing hours of operation. When it first began, the house was open from 8:00 A.M. until 5:00 P.M., five days a week. Six months later, residents insisted that it remain open from 8:00 A.M. until 9:00 P.M., five days a week. At this writing, residents have decided the house should remain open from 8:00 A.M. until 9:30 P.M. during the work week, and all day Saturday and Sunday. Informally, the house is usually open after official closing time. Furthermore, the neighborhood staff are considered, by residents, to be on call 24 hours a day.

Approximately 20 meetings a week are held at the neighborhood house, including the following classes: youth and adult education, cooking, sewing, health, hat-making, gardening, landscaping, and arts and crafts. Weekly neighborhood meetings are held, encouraging relaxed informal discussion concerning neighborhood needs, problems, and activities. Each month the original Highland Park-Pierce Neighborhood Committee conducts its official meeting in the house. An increasing number of impromptu get-togethers form in the house as it becomes "the place to meet."

When asked for whom he worked, the house director inevitably would respond "for us, for the Neighborhood people." When he had been an extension worker, the director felt that he had to "meet the needs of the agency more than the needs of the people." Now he was more clearly able to identify with those whom he served. During his first encounters with agency officials as director of the neighborhood house, he tended to be suspicious of their motives and somewhat defensive. For example, often he would appear in an official's office without an appointment, hoping to "catch them off guard" and not give "the opposition a chance to dig in and maintain its defenses." His early philosophy, as described by the director, was "attack rather that tact." However, with experience the director realized that "hostility got me hostility in return." Advised by the house social worker, he concentrated on the structure and procedures of the agencies, and became acquainted with some areas of flexibility within the organizational systems. Gradually the director came to interpret an agency response of, "That's impossible," to mean "You've got to try a new way." When he would discover a way in which an agency could render an innovative service to someone in the neighborhood, the agency officials, as reported by the director, would "be thankful as hell. Some of those guys are as happy as we are when someone points out to them a new way to use their own system." The director became less willing to impute malevolent motivation to agency officials, and more prone to assess realistically the useful but complex and sometimes self-defeating nature of bureaucratic procedure. He saw the neighborhood house staff, along with those whom he accepted as colleagues in the service organizations, as faced with the task of "using the system to our best advantage."

On occasion, though he identified himself clearly with the target neighborhood residents, the director experienced stresses of marginality — of being a bridge between the poor and not-poor. He felt pressured by conflicting expectations for his performance by neighborhood residents on the one hand, and agency officials on the other. (For other discussions of conflicts and stresses experienced by indigenous nonprofessionals, see: Grosser, 1966; Reiff & Riessman, 1965; Zurcher, 1967b.) As he became more expert in "playing the role" in an agency setting, and more resourceful in reaching and effectively helping neighborhood residents, the director became more tolerant of his often marginal operating position. He philosophized that stresses resulting from conflicting expectations for his performance were "just part of the job."

The role model and informal training provided by the house's social worker from the supporting agency profoundly influenced the director's effectiveness with agency representatives. Similarly, the role model and informal training provided by the director profoundly influenced the social worker's effectiveness with neighborhood residents. At first guardedly but soon openly they shared with each other frustrations, satisfactions and strategies associated with social innovation. This sharing erased

earlier feelings each had that the other "might just con him."
The evolution of their relationship, and consequently the evolution of the relationship between neighborhood house and
supporting agency, demonstrated the feasibility of indigenous
leaders and organizations working closely and beneficially with
professional leaders and organizations—as long as experiences
can be shared by functional equals in a cooperative rather than
competitive climate.

Chapter 4

Creating a Neighborhood

PRIOR to the creation of the house, Highland Park-Pierce seemed to be a neighborhood primarily because of city-determined geographical boundaries and a relatively unstable sense of out-group cohesion — "This is one of the areas where us Negroes can live." There was no neighborhood in the organized, purposive, or self-determined connotation of the word. Initially, as indicated above, the house staff was committed to facilitating services for needy residents in a dignified fashion. The house staff had no systematized thoughts about organizing the neighborhood or neighborhood groups for social action. Similarly, residents were initially most concerned about what the house could do for them, not what they could do for themselves in organized groups through the house.

By the end of November, 1966, the beginnings of group organization toward social change goals could be observed. About 30 residents had decided they wanted an unstructured neighborhood meeting on the last Thursday of every month.

This meeting was open to all members of the neighborhood, and was to be without agenda or designated chairman. Discussions were to be concerned with whatever the attending participants would at the time see fit to discuss. At one of those meetings, a resident suggested to the group, "Let's get out into the neighborhood, the bunch of us, and do something together. I mean something constructive and not just a picnic or a party." The participants seemed responsive to that idea, and after some discussion agreed that a suitable first project would be to "get out as a group and clean up some of these weed-ridden yards and empty lots that make our blocks look like slums." Another resident recommended that the man who had made the suggestion to clean lots be established as chairman of the Cleanup Committee. The chairman-nominee audibly choked and exclaimed "Me! I've never done anything like that before! I can't be a chairman! I can't lead that thing!" His wife vehemently agreed, saying, "Yeah, that's right! He can't do that! He's never done nothing like that!" After considerable encouragement from other members of the group, the chairman-nominee agreed, and became the chairman-elect. On several Saturdays thereafter, he convened his small work force, ranging from 4 to 12 men at pre-chosen work sites. Volunteers would chop and rake weeds, gather and haul litter, and when finished, plant a sign which stated "This Lot Cleared by the Highland Park-Pierce Neighborhood House." Though the chairman had difficulty "keeping the work crew bigger in size than just me," several lots were improved. As a result of their example, a number of other families spontaneously cleared weeds from their own yards. Most important, however, was the fact that the work was the first, the precedent-setting, spontaneous organization of neighborhood residents — through the house — toward an agreed upon group goal.

Several of the committees and classes meeting regularly in the neighborhood house evolved toward broader goals than those for which they were first intended. One committee, for example, was begun by residents to seek new ways to help senior citizens. Shortly, however, consideration of the problems of senior citizens expanded to consideration of the problems of the neighborhood residents as a whole. The meetings became general forums on social problems. Regular attendance grew to 40 members, not necessarily because the group was resolving issues at that time, but because it gave members a chance to define those issues, in many cases for the first time in their lives. The topics for their discussions began to crystallize. Subgroups were formed to deal with more specific problems, and to develop action toward solutions. The subcommittees were concerned with politics, recreation, employment, legislative change, and education. Representatives of the subcommittees consulted with city officials who could advise them on matters relative to their interests, problems, and proposals. Subsequently, this forum replaced the monthly neighborhood house business meetings, thus affording an opportunity for continuous community dialogue and a staging ground for neighborhood-based social action.

The chairman of the Highland Park-Pierce Neighborhood Committee, expressing the feelings of the membership at a current meeting, spoke of "the importance of our rehabilitating our neighborhood." Somewhat fearful of urban renewal and stimulated by the changes in the landscape brought about by the Cleanup Committee, residents began talking about what they could do "to make our neighborhood a proudful place." That sense of neighborhood was further sharpened by the community-wide publicity, in the form of newspaper feature stories, editorials and television reports, that Highland Park-Pierce was receiving through the activities of its new neighborhood house. Through the various programs, classes, services, and field activities of the house, residents were interacting more frequently and in new ways with one another. "I was reminded of the old days," reflected an 82-year-old man who was among the first residents of the area.

We all used to get together down at the general store. We would sit around and talk, and share our troubles with one another, and go out and do things together if they had to be done. That kind of store isn't around here anymore, but the Neighborhood House sure seems just like one, except they don't sell you nothing.

The neighborhood house seemed to be beginning to function as a focal point for neighborhood integration.

Increasingly, residents themselves emphasized the need for neighborhood organization. "What makes a big voice," proclaimed a participant in the monthly neighborhood meeting, "is not one man screaming all alone. It's a hundred voices together. That's what is heard!" Other participants commented less graphically about "the strength of organization for getting things done." The potential for political and economic organization was acknowledged and specific measures, such as voter registration and credit unions, were discussed.

The director, continuing to be influenced by the desire of residents, similarly began to see the neighborhood house as being able to fulfill a purpose beyond helping specific individuals in a nonthreatening way. "I am getting the feeling," he commented,

> that at first the House was really only able to hand out band-aids to people one at a time, when what was really needed was a transfusion for the whole Neighborhood. The services, when they are gotten in the right way, are necessary, and we're going to continue taking advantage of them. But if poverty and inequality are really going to be ended here, we're going to have to change two things. First, our image as "no good poverty types" and second, the parts of the system that support poverty and inequality. You can do both those things with responsible people organized. I think we are getting that kind of organization out here.

In June, 1967, neighborhood residents suggested to the house staff that a weekly newsletter be published and distributed as "another way to let us communicate with one another." The staff acted upon the suggestion, and each week prepared a mimeographed newsletter listing house and general activities, schedules, volunteer services, wanted or for sale items, rentals, babysitting services, etc. The letters are distributed to each home in the neighborhood by children of the residents. Five weeks after its first distribution, the newsletter was much in demand, evidenced by the number of telephone calls of concern when for one reason or another the paper was a day late or missing. Furthermore, a number of community residents immediately outside the boundaries of Highland Park-Pierce have requested that the newsletter be delivered to them, as well as to residents inside the boundaries. The implementation of and reaction to the Highland Park-Pierce Newsletter seems to manifest a growing perception of a cohesive neighborhood.

The content of the newsletter indicated the broadening scope of neighborhood house functioning. The publication announced newly available services, listed personal announcements and other "newsy" items. In addition, however, as revealed in the sample presented below, the newsletter editorialized on civil rights legislation, stimulated concern about public housing and voter registration, and reported the director's action concerning the city's proposed Model Police Force. The concept of a united neighborhood making concerted efforts toward social action was becoming explicit.

HIGHLAND PARK-PIERCE NEWSLETTER

More Needs to be Done!

Many people in America have been forced to do some serious thinking about the many citizens living in ghettos in our cities. However, there hasn't been a demand by all the people, unamimously (sic), to enact laws—for programs of the poor. The federal government has only made a beginning which instead of staisfying (sic) the need has only intensified our realization of the large gap between what has been done and what needs to be done. This was recognized in a statement by the National Committee of Negro Churchmen in July of 1966: "We submit that to pass a Civil Rights Bill as this nation did in 1875 and then refuse to enforce it; to pass another Civil Rights Bill (weaker this time) in 1964 and then refuse to enforce it; to begin an anti-poverty program with insufficient funds in the first place and then to put the lion's share of this miniscule budget into Head Start programs when unemployment among Negro men continues to skyrocket; to declare segregation in our schools unconstitutional as the Supreme Court did in 1954, and then refuse to end it forthwith; to set up guidelines for desegregating hospitals and then refuse to appropriate money for the enforcement of these guidelines; to insist on civil rights legislation aimed at the south and then to defeat the first piece of such legislation relevant to areas outside the south; to preach "law and order" into the anguish of Negro slums in full view of the contributions of policemen to that anguish and then to insist that policemen be their own judges; to hear the suburban politicians declaim against open occupancy in one breath and in the very next breath insist that they are not racists: These are the ironies which stare us in the face and make it all but impossible to talk about how much "progress" has been made. The fact of the matter is if black Americans are not accorded basic human and constitutional rights which white Americans gain immediately upon their entry into citizenship, then there really are no substantive gains of which to speak.

The Aniversary (sic) Dinner went over real big! The officers of three other areas were here as guests. They were Mr. Wayne Barber, Lowman Hill; Mr. and Mrs. Ralph Ulm of North Topeka East; Mrs. Ann Newman and Mrs. Delsi of East Topeka.

Washburn University has agreed to use the Neighborhood House as a field training agency. There will be two seniors assigned starting with the fall seminster (sic). These students will be under the supervision of the Neighborhood House Staff. They will be used to help families dealing with the existing agencies. They will be carefully chosen to fit the needs of our community but we must cooperate to insure getting the best services the agencies have to offer.

The limited public housing is fast becoming a reality. If you have any questions in this regard, please call CE 5-6214 or CE 5-6215.

Mrs. Ferguson deserves many thanks for the research on the voter registration in our community!

The Teen-age Activity Group will meet again Tuesday night from 7-9 P.M. This is a chance for teen-agers to participate in supervised activity.

Elizabeth Munoz, secretary at the Neighborhood House is leaving this Friday for a position as a secretary on the staff of Governor Docking. Elizabeth has been an able and engaging member of our staff and we will miss her very much. We wish her all the success in the future!

The cooking and sewing class held a farewell party for Mrs. Munoz. Mrs. Munoz cooked tostados for the ladies. Attending were Mrs. Mae Shazier; Mrs. Indiola Blount; Mrs. Pauline Johnson, Mrs. Betty Mitchell, Mrs. Camille Crim, Mrs. JoAnn Martin, Miss Rosetta Byrd, Miss Elizabeth Boltz and Mrs. Munoz.

BIRTHDAY PARTY: Maurice & Dorothy Netherland celebrated their birthdays at a party at the Neighborhood House. Attending were: Dorothy, Maurice, Donald, Evelyn, Gwen, Lenora, Lillian and Katherine Netherland, Lavirtes, Dorian and Carla Martin.

Adult Education classes will continue on Wednesday Nights through the month of August beginning at 7:30 P.M. Last Wednesday, a reading test was given.

This gest (sic) will help you know where to begin reading improvement. Those that missed the class are urged to drop by and take the test at the center any time during the day. New members in the class are: Mrs. Maxine Law, Mrs. Norma Brisco, Mrs. Georgia Kirtdoll, Mr. & Mrs. Stuart Porter, Mr. & Mrs. Lawrence Irish.

The Neighborhood House now has two new telephone lines. The new numbers are CE 5-6214 and CE 5-6215. We want to be more available for communication.

The *Bookmobile* comes by the Neighborhood House on Wednesday mornings at 10:00 and leaves at 11:00 A.M. This service will continue through August and we hope a schedule can be set up for the regular school year beginning in September. Plenty of adult books are available — mysteries, novels, cook books, household books, books on the bible.

Rev. E. E. Kirtdoll announced the following times for Sunday Services:

    Sunday School — 9:30 A.M.
    Worship   — 11:00 A.M.

Mr. Ed Johnson went on record by writing the City Commissioners opposing the increase in Police Force according to the Model Police Plan. Says Mr. Johnson, "First, we need to take steps toward having a Model City, like getting better roads. Then we can think about a Model Police Force!"

Mrs. Olivia Burden gave birth to a daughter, Shelia, on July 22, 1967.

Mrs. Ann Garvin is in need of transportation for her children to and from Highland Park Central School daily when school begins. She would also need about two hours per day of child care for them. Anyone interested may call the Neighborhood House for further information: CE 5-6214 or CE 6-6215.

"Action, Together!"

With an increase in neighborhood identity, several residents became more convinced of the importance of rehabilitating and maintaining the neighborhood as a residential area. They did not want Highland Park-Pierce to be considered a slum section. The residents were aware of the need for better streets, more adequate lighting, more efficient sewage disposal, and for the provision of adequate low-cost housing. But they seemed fearful of compulsory urban renewal in which plans would be made for them, independent of the neighborhood's own involvement and needs. As a result of this concern and an increased appreciation of neighborhood, for the first time in Topeka's history a low-income area began to work under its own stimulation and initiation for urban development which could be funded by a cooperative city and federal program. In December, 1966, the residents invited the director of urban renewal to meet with them at the neighborhood house, and to discuss ways for "us to rehabilitate our neighborhood." The residents were not discouraged by the complexities of city, state and federal urban renewal policies as explained to them. A number of residents, including the neighborhood house staff, have now become familiar with urban renewal legislation, what can and cannot be accomplished by implementation of the law, and participant responsibilities in the planning and development of local projects. Though no operational plan has yet been evolved by Highland Park-Pierce residents through governmental channels, they continue efforts toward acquiring official recognition of their desire to rehabilitate the neighborhood at their own direction and without arbitrary relocation.

The house staff and the Target Neighborhood Committee are presently launched upon a campaign to stimulate: (1) rehabilitation of blighted but serviceable homes; (2) destruction and clearing of homes already condemned; (3) the building of new homes in the neighborhood—"building homes in a low-income area is a good investment"; (4) rent subsidy or the building of low rental units; (5) the development of a class on "how to take care of property"; (6) the establishing of a neighborhood housing corporation to be run by Highland Park-Pierce residents. At one of their meetings, residents concluded "Our neighborhood has the highest potential of all the others in Shawnee County. We've got more and better land available than anywhere else. Let's find better ways to use it, or else we're liable to lose it."

Later in December, residents took advantage of an opportunity to reinforce their consensus about rehabilitating and maintaining Highland Park-Pierce as a residential area. By their action they demonstrated to the community-at-large that they identified with their neighborhood, and wished to "have some say" about changes that were made within it.

A local service station owner wanted to expand his business by building a branch in Highland Park-Pierce. He had located suitable property, and had filed a request with the City Commission for rezoning the property from residential to commercial designation. The neighborhood house staff, in their routine review of published city business, learned of the businessman's intention and took it to the neighborhood residents for discussion. After considerable debate and deliberation, the residents unanimously agreed that commercial rezoning would not be compatible with their goals for residential rehabilitation. The residents directed the neighborhood house staff to send the following letter to the Board of City Commissioners:

Board of City Commissioners
City Building
Topeka, Kansas
Gentlemen:

This letter is written in behalf of the people of the Highland Park-Pierce Neighborhood in protest of rezoning the corner of 25th & Adams for a service station.

It is the feeling of the Advisory Board that such a step would be a detriment to the area and would be in direct opposition to what we are trying to achieve in the way of bettering the neighborhood and general surroundings for the neighborhood people. Commercial zoning would mean encouragement of other types of business nearby, and thus, lower the property value and at the same time lessen the hope of developing this area into a desirable residential neighborhood.

The general feeling of those who live in this area is unfavorable toward rezoning and they have submitted protest thru petitions.

Your consideration in this matter will be greatly appreciated.

As follow-up to the letter, 35 neighborhood residents attended a subsequent meeting of the Board of Commissioners at City Hall, and verbally registered their objections to the rezoning.

In order to give the businessman an opportunity to explain his application, the neighborhood residents invited him to meet with them in the Highland Park-Pierce Neighborhood House. The businessman told the attending residents and neighborhood house staff that his studies and discussions with commissioners showed that, within five to ten years, the street on which he wished to build his new service station would be a major thoroughfare, and would be zoned commercially. He talked about the advantages of having a service station in the area, and passed around a picture of one of his stations in a middle-class section of town. His major arguments were that the service station would complement the neighborhood and that eventually the property would be rezoned anyway.

When he had finished his presentation, residents expressed their specific objections. Some felt that the establishment of a service station would lower the property value of surrounding houses. Others felt that one service station would bring with it a proliferation of service stations, and associated noise unsuitable to a residential area. A Negro woman worried that a service station would bring in the "motorcycle crowd." One of the men systematically pointed to the number of service stations readily accessible in the nearby shopping and business areas, and wondered why one had to be put up in the middle of their "living places."

The businessman reiterated his argument that change was going to take place inevitably, and that progress shouldn't be stopped. The chairman of the Target Neighborhood Committee responded:

> We know the area will develop. We want it to. There is growth all around us. We know this. We want to develop with the rest of the City, but we feel we want to develop our Neighborhood as we see fit. Now, if you're willing to help our Neighborhood as you say, then you should be willing to see our point. You are interested in the Neighborhood for your station's sake; we are interested in the Neighborhood for the Neighborhood's sake. We know that street will be a major thoroughfare someday, and we know that major thoroughfares offer good commercial sites. But we would like to keep our area strictly residential, and develop it into a place where people can be proud to live.

The businessman stated he thought he would have a good chance for building the station even if the people didn't agree, but added "I'm going to withdraw my application for the rezoning. I don't want to offend you; I would want your business." He then stated,

> I have a proposition for you to consider. Would you review this request, say, in another two or three years? It may be that you will be willing to have a station then.

The chairman of the Target Neighborhood Committee responded.

> Sir, I have a proposition for you. Would you be willing to help us plan the development of our Neighborhood in the way that we would like to have it, and in a way that would be beneficial to all?

The businessman accepted, and the session adjourned. After the meeting, one of the neighborhood residents told the businessman that he had

> made a mistake. You shouldn't have bought the land, requested a rezoning permit, and then told the people about it. You should have come to us first, and you could have saved yourself that trouble.

Neighborhood residents, as a result of their experience with the rezoning case, had the opportunity to learn more about the workings of "the system" in the community, and the effective means to communicate desires within that system. More important, residents were now convinced, by the success of their own action, that "people, no matter how poor, can get something done if they act together." Through petition, personal appearances, and direct confrontation with the issues, the residents had influenced the "unbeatable power structure." The "system" seemed to them far less formidable now, far less alien. With a strong case rationally and forcefully presented by numbers, residents had observed that decisions made by representatives of the establishment did not necessarily have to be arbitrary decisions. From firsthand experience of the workings of complex social structures, residents were gaining insight concerning how the structures affect them and, more importantly, how they could affect the structures. Their subsequent encounters, some successful and some unsuccessful, with powers before believed to be unapproachable and unmovable seemed to yield increasing self-confidence and a sense of competency and power.

After their success in blocking the rezoning attempt, residents launched upon a series of endeavors toward neighborhood improvement. They petitioned the City Commission for increased attention to "our non-roads in Highland Park-Pierce." They requested that additional street lights be installed in their neighborhood. They approached the Fire Department and asked them to raze the deserted houses that had previously been condemned by the city. Representatives of the neighborhood house volunteered testimony in support of a controversial minimum housing code under review by the City Commission. The neighborhood house staff, at the prompting of residents, registered disillusionment with the city's attempt to implement a "Model Police Program" when, in their view, "first we ought to take steps toward having a Model City, and try to eliminate the social problems which cause police problems." A committee from the house approached the State Legislature, requesting a change of law that would broaden the existing cosmetology training program, making it more accessible and useful to residents. Each of those social action endeavors was conducted in an orderly, purposive, but united manner. The outcome of most of these attempts is still pending, but residents, aware of their new found "clout," are steadily maintaining pressure to get what they think is best for themselves and the neighborhood.

As action evolved, so also did a new set of stated goals for the neighborhood house. The first set of goals, developed by the Topeke OEO, Advisory Council, and some neighborhood residents stressed facilitation of services. The second set of goals (borrowed from Reissman & Hallowitz, 1967) stressed more centrally purposive social change:

1. to provide psychosocial first aid to large numbers of people experiencing stress from both external and internal causes;
2. to transform passive, uninvolved, apathetic, receivers of

others' beneficence into helpers and active citizens;

3. to develop independence, autonomy, and better overall functioning on the part of the people in the neighborhood;

4. to demonstrate that indigenous nonprofessionals can provide meaningful service for their population;

5. to initiate changes in services—emphasizing the importance of the impact of the helper on the helped;

6. to affect the neighborhood by developing greater social integration and cohesion among the residents.

"Rub Out the Imaginary Boundaries"

Initially, as the neighborhood house began to develop, residents were concerned about what the programs could do for them as individuals. As a sense of neighborhood grew, residents began to experience the value of group efforts toward social action that would have impact upon Highland Park-Pierce. Increase of self-initiated contacts with agencies and involvement in concerted social action seemed to generate among participating residents a new realization of their dignity, worth, and potency. Reinforced by their now demonstrated competencies and strengthened by awareness of membership in a cohesive neighborhood, the participants were willing to extend themselves beyond their own turf. The experience of ownership of and responsibility for self and neighborhood began to generalize to the community-at-large.

At a recent neighborhood meeting, the participants discussed "the role of the neighborhood house in the city of Topeka." Whereas they agreed that the house's first obligation was to Highland Park-Pierce, they also agreed that

we should be neighbors to everyone in the City of Topeka. We should be willing to help anyone who needs it, whether he is black or white. We have a problem with poverty, but so does the City of Topeka. We should share what we have learned about poverty, the hard way, with those who really want to do something about it.

Some of the social action with which residents had already been involved concerned the community-at-large — for example, their support of the Minimum Housing Code for the City of Topeka, their statements in support of the Model City program, and their criticism of the Model Police project. The director's letter to the City Commissioners regarding the Model Police project reflects both neighborhood and city concern.

Board of City Commissioners
City Building
Topeka, Kansas

Gentlemen :
While we would be the first to defend better wages and working conditions for all public employees, whether he be policeman or fireman, we cannot support the "Model Police program." The proponents of this program may have overlooked the kind of city they are hoping to police.

We wonder where these police advocates were when there was some mild discussion going on about a "Model City." It would seem that the two should grow together. If we hope to have a city that warrants expansion of police protection, it would be necessary to improve all areas of service. If streets were improved in some areas of the city, a policeman may be able to get to a troubled spot faster and thereby eliminate the need to hire new ones. The police have done a good job in the past in keeping a close watch on the deprived, denied and neglected areas of our city. Is it obvious that these are situations which will continue and the need to control these elements are growing? If so, where will it end? We would ask the City Commission and those who have defended this model police program to examine other possibilities of making the City of Topeka a better place to live for all.

The police problem is mild compared to other needs. This approach will not solve the problems. We respect the opinions of these will (sic) meaning citizens but we don't think they understand the seriousness of the other problems. The kind of problems that would dictate the need for such expert police department, as has been proposed, should be given first consideration. It is believed here, that the "Model Police" without a "Model City" would only serve a few for a short while.

Twenty of the 42 students in the adult education program conducted at the house are from areas outside Highland Park-Pierce. A day-care center has been established in the neighborhood, and students have been invited from other neighborhoods.

The Highland Park-Pierce residents' emphasis upon neighborhood rehabilitation rather than relocation emphasized potential benefit for Topeka. "Improving and increasing residential property in our neighborhood would be a benefit to the city," suggested a resident.

> Then they would be able to get more tax revenue that way. Right now, they're only getting farm taxes from right here in the middle of the city. They could use that extra tax money for better streets and more lighting in Highland Park-Pierce, but also for other areas too.

Plans for the house's anniversary party included an open invitation to "all citizens of Topeka." "We want to let everyone know that we are developing our neighborhood, but we are not developing it like an island," exclaimed the director. The Neighborhood Committee Chairman agreed, adding,

> We need the help of other people in Topeka, there is no question about that. But we have also learned now that the people of Topeka need our help in meeting this poverty problem. It's time we rub out the imaginary boundaries between us.

A number of citizens in the community-at-large asked the house to schedule meetings in which problems of poverty and prejudice could be discussed with city-wide participation. The house responded and, at 7:30 P.M. on August 22, the first meeting of "Let's Talk" was held. For three hours, 30 participants, black and white, poor and not-poor, discussed issues relevant to "a movement toward better racial understanding." The meeting, described by a newspaper reporter as having "never really ended," was thereafter regularly held each Monday night in the neighborhood house.

In August, the house director had manifested his and residents' widening concept of community responsibility. He learned from some of the residents that "trouble was about to begin" in another part of the city. Some Negro workingmen had been subject to what they felt were unilateral and unfair work changes, resulting in a loss of accumulated vacation time without compensation. Thinking that they had no other way to express their grievances, and stimulated by some current violent activity in poverty areas of larger cities, the men decided to "mess up the landscape a little bit." The house director, agreeing with Highland Park-Pierce residents that he "should try to do something about it," rushed to the area and "let the guys know there might be a better way to solve their problems than getting people hurt." The director, who had years before been a member of a corner gang in the same area, convinced the men to "try it my way first, and if that doesn't work, then do what you want." The director and the men met with the employers, presented the grievances, and worked out a solution satisfactory to all. Several Topeka citizens credit the director's action as having "prevented the beginning of a riot."

Successful and recognized involvement in city-wide affairs seemed further to enhance the identities of the participants and to increase the number of their functional social roles. Residents increasingly commented about "our community" as well as "our neighborhood." The growing feeling of belongingness and responsibility was perhaps best exemplified by the following statement, made by the chairman of the Highland Park-Pierce Neighborhood Committee as he reflected upon two years of involvement in the poverty program:

I sometimes wonder how I got involved in all this! People ask me how I got started, and I really can't give a very good answer. I can only say that no other program has made such an impression on me in all my life.

It's hard for me to explain. Maybe it's that it's hard for a Negro man to find a place in the mainstream of the society. But now I have a feeling that I have found a slot in life for myself. This program offered me an opportunity to create that slot that I have been looking for maybe all my life. I was a pretty quiet guy, never wanting to get into the limelight. I always wanted to stay out of the way, because it was safer that way. I'm in a position now where I can really help other people, and I can see the results of my work and it makes me feel good. It makes me feel that I am really somebody. Sure, there are still people who I depend upon for help. Everybody needs somebody. But now I can see that others need me, too—people in the Neighborhood and people in Topeka.

I'm listened to with respect now in some places that maybe wouldn't have let me through their door two years ago. They don't always agree with me, but I wouldn't want that either. What's important is that people now think that me, and the people I represent, are worth listening to. That makes you feel worth more. Makes you feel more like a man. These last two years of happiness in the program, of being able to find myself, have been worth more than all my other adult years.

Chapter 5

Community Response

A S a result of their experiences with the neighborhood
house, at least the participating residents appeared to
be altering perceptions of themselves, the neighborhood, the
"system," and the community-at-large. Members of the system
and the community-at-large seemed correspondingly to be altering their views of Highland Park-Pierce and its residents.
Personnel from agencies and service organizations with whom
the neighborhood house staff interacted, noticeably and rather
quickly, shifted to a colleague relationship with the house
director. Increasingly, representatives from such agencies as
County Welfare, Family Service and Guidance, Urban Renewal,
Public Health, Board of Education, and Small Business Loan
Association called upon the neighborhood house staff not
only for reciprocal services, but for advice and consultation
concerning case problems. For example, some of the local
schools were experiencing difficulties with a few of their students
from low-income areas and were unsuccessful in recruiting

parents' efforts toward resolving the problems. The schools contacted the neighborhood house for suggestions about ways to engage the parents successfully. In response, the house staff reviewed in detail with school officials the feelings that some low-income parents have toward the school system, particularly with regard to meeting teachers and administrative officials. The director further explained that whereas school officials often imputed "lack of motivation" to low-income parents, some low-income parents imputed a lack of "real helping" motivation to the school officials. The house staff suggested that the house serve as a place where parents and officials could meet. In this way the residents, on their own turf, could feel more comfortable, secure, and perhaps more confident. Furthermore, the school officials would openly demonstrate their desire to be helpful by having "come out of those big offices." The procedure proved to be quite successful, and subsequently other agencies availed themselves of the same opportunity for direct contact with low-income people in a nonthreatening environment. Not only were the anxieties of the residents often reduced, thereby making possible their freer use of agency facilities, but simultaneously an educational process developed for the agency personnel themselves. Less frequently one heard statements citing lack of motivation, apathy, lack of involvement, etc. Agency personnel found their successful encounters with residents who had previously been difficult to reach surprising and gratifying. Many officials verbally expressed appreciation of the neighborhood house's efforts. More importantly, their operating policies expanded to include consultation with the neighborhood house.

The neighborhood house and the neighborhood that owned it became recognized as a serious enterprise. One-way channels of information became two-way channels for communication. The neighborhood house was becoming a respected member of the fraternity of legitimized community formal organizations.

The house staff received several letters from citizens outside Highland Park-Pierce. Most of the letters congratulated the house on various activities, and wished the staff and residents well in their future pursuits. One letter congratulated the house staff for its stand on a city issue, even though the writer didn't "agree with all you had to say." Another writer thanked "the people of Highland Park-Pierce for taking an interest in the City." A third citizen: "Just wanted to drop you a line and thank you for making Highland Park-Pierce a more beautiful place to drive through. Whenever I had visitors from out of town I used to avoid driving through the area. . .."

Local Press Stimulates Interest

The local newspapers stimulated and reflected community interest in and appreciation of the Highland Park-Pierce Neighborhood House. Fifteen news stories about the house have appeared in the Topeka newspaper since its opening. Some of the headlines and/or captions read: "Topeka's First Neighborhood House Dedicated By Officials," *Topeka Daily Capitol*, October, 1966; "Blighted Areas Cleaned. . .Cleanup Job is Launched," *Topeka State Journal*, November, 1966; "Highland Park-Pierce Neighborhood House Run By The Neighborhood," *Highland Park-Pierce and South Topeka News*, January, 1967; "Topeka Community Now Finding Leaders," *Topeka Daily Capitol*, May, 1967; "OEO And Police Argue On Plan," *The Pictorial Times*, January, 1967; "Student Helps Prepare Pupils For GED Test. . .Session In The Highland Park-Pierce Neighborhood House," *Topeka Daily Capitol*, August, 1967; "Negroes, Whites Starting Dialogue," *Topeka Daily Capitol*, August, 1967; "Bookmobile Plans Two New Stops," *Topeka State Journal*, September, 1967; "Minority Jobs Are Discussed," *Topeka State Journal*, September, 1967; "'Talk' Group Plans Action," *Topeka Daily Capitol*, September, 1967.

To illustrate further the sensitive reporting by local press and the growing recognition of the neighborhood house's beneficial functioning, the following article is presented *in toto:*

TOPEKA COMMUNITY NOW FINDING LEADERS

By Bert Rinkel

There are streets in the center of Topeka which are muddy when the rains fall, and whipped with dust when the sun shines. Streets in the Highland Park-Pierce area are not only thoroughfares; they are also barriers.

The broken houses and rough, unpaved streets are hidden from motorists driving near the area bounded by Kansas Avenue on the west, Ohio to the east, 17th and Interstate 70 to the north and 29th on the south.

As the two men walked, they talked about their efforts to create leadership and understanding of problems within the Highland Park-Pierce community.

They explained how they had worked with Topeka's poverty program, the Office of Economic Opportunity, to find people within the area who understood their problems best and were willing to work for a change.

Since the beginning of the Highland Park-Pierce Target Neighborhood Committee two years ago and the founding of the Neighborhood House last year, Patton, Johnson and other persons have worked to get the area's streets improved.

The two men told how the leadership in the community was trying to demonstrate to Topeka that people there do want to work for a better environment. They told how persons there were becoming convinced for the first time that the situation could change.

"The people here know that the leaders are not from the outside. Both Sam and I live in the community. Respect and dignity and concern for the community comes when the people within feel they can make their own decisions," Johnson said.

"That's what we're working for. We may need the help of some outside funds, but the first problem is to create a spirit and dignity from within," he said.

Two children played in front of a wood-frame house which tilted to one side on its foundation. A scrap of tarpaper was tugged and flapped by the afternoon wind.

Johnson, director of the Highland Park-Pierce Neighborhood House, 515 E. 25th, kicked a stone into a ditch alongside the road.

"About 1,200 persons live in the Highland Park-Pierce area," he said. "An estimated 70 percent of the residents are Negro. One-third of them are poverty stricken," he said.

"The really hard-core area is the Pierce addition. It has had the potential of being a ghetto since 1902. In the area from 17th to 20th and from Kansas Avenue to Adams, 90 percent of the residents are Negro," he said.

"But you can't read this off as a way of life. It's not an incurable disease. We're trying to develop some kind of approach to meet our needs in this community," he said.

Patton, Chairman of the Highland Park-Pierce Neighborhood Committee of the Topeka Office of Economic Opportunity, said most of the streets in the 15-square block area had not been paved and there are no street lights.

However, Patton said he and his committee had worked for two years to have the community improved.

Two weeks ago, city street employees started to grade the streets and street lights have been promised for the area.

The problem of streets has symbolized the community's dilemma.

Patton said the residents couldn't pay the taxes necessary for fully-paved streets. They approached the city officials about their problem. "For a long time, we got the runaround," he said. "At first we thought we could get asphalt — not concrete-paving. But now they say the law will only allow the use of a light oil coat which will be gone in a year," he said.

Oil and New Houses

The two men continued to walk the streets of the Pierce area. A well-built, freshly painted house stood next to a shack with siding peeling off the walls.

Along asphalt-paved Adams Street — dividing Pierce from Highland Park, a row of fairly new homes lined one side of the street. On the other, stood a ramshackle home with an old car in front.

Johnson pointed at the contrasting homes. "One side of the street makes a world of difference in your income," he said.

The two men stood in silence for a moment. "No, I don't have all the statistics on the problems of the area," Johnson said. "We've been studied until it is almost a joke. But if there is one outdoor privy — that's too many."

"We're beginning to learn that we're not helpless — we can make changes in our community," Patton said. "But many of the people here don't have the education or the skills to get better jobs. It's not true that they don't want to work. No one likes welfare and the way it can degrade a man," he said.

"Yet, those who have the skills are faced with employers who won't hire them because of their color," he said. "And sometimes a man may have the money, but the color of his skin keeps him from buying a house he wants," Patton said.

"Another problem is getting a loan. I've checked, and it's almost impossible to get a bank loan for a house in this area," he said.

"Second, we hope we can get Urban Renewal to improve the homes. There are grants for low-income homeowners. We could build low-cost homes and apartments on the vacant lots without moving anybody," Patton said.

Marked Children

"You have to also realize what happens to a child — and how it marks him as a man."

"Children that leave this segregated area are afraid of a biracial school. It would be terrible if they were segregated, but people don't realize the really physical fear that a Negro can feel at times — and just because he's been seggregated by the system," Patton said.

Patton stopped and looked at one of the many vacant lots in the area. It was a tangle of weeds and rubbish.

"This hurts the city, too," he said. "They're getting farmland taxes in the middle of the city."

Action Needed

"The problem is, we have to have Urban Renewal projects in other parts of the city besides downtown. You have to have action beyond the inspections," he said.

The two men turned around in the road and started up a hill. The Capitol dome appeared on the horizon. The hill sloped down to Shunganunga Creek and the railroad tracks.

Patton tapped his hand against his side. "Overall, we're involving people in a program that will get something done."

"First, we need job training programs. You see a lot of homes where the mother can make more than the father. The kids don't have fathers they can look to. The man of the house is frustrated."

Frustrated People

"That's one reason for the outbreaks of violence and crime here sometimes. People are frustrated by the inequities of the system. They've had their bootstraps cut off too many times."

Johnson and Patton reached the top of the hill and looked down at Lakewood Park.

"There are other things. We don't have a recreation center in this area."

"We went to the city commission and asked them to improve the ball diamond at the park. They said they couldn't because the Girl Scouts had an option to camp out there. We're trying to get that changed," he said.

A man walked from his home and approached the two men.

Garbage Problem

"Sam, can we work something out about garbage collection? Couldn't we put the cans in the alley instead of out on the streets?" he asked.

"Let's call the city sanitation department and see what can be done," Patton replied.

Johnson and Patton walked further down the road. An empty house, it's windows gone, was slowly deteriorating back to the earth.

"The city forgets this area. Take that house. It was placarded by the city. That means they're supposed to tear it down. It's been that way two years now," Johnson said.

"The house is a bridge between the people and an agency that might help them. A lot of middle-class people know how to go to somebody and get help. Many people here don't know how or don't believe they can," he said.

As an example, Johnson told how the community through the neighborhood house stopped the construction of a service station between two homes. The mothers were afraid of the extra traffic as their children went to school.

The residents went to a zoning hearing, met with the person wanting to build the station, and the station was not constructed.

"It was a vivid demonstration to the people of what we can do," he said.

A car stopped by the two men. The woman driving the car said, "If you're taking a survey, we've got some things we need help with. Come on over."

The car drove on.

"We have about 100 per cent support from the community together. People here today are talking about what they can do. Two years ago, they thought the situation was hopeless," Johnson said.

"Even before OEO—Topeka's poverty program—started, the residents of the area formed a community improvement committee Patton said.

"When the OEO Target Neighborhood Committee started, people wanted to work for better streets first of all," he said.

The area residents went to the city commission. "After two years, we may finally get something done," Patton said.

"First of all, the house is run by people in the neighborhood. We hope to see things done, because we know our problems. We have seen too many promises and no action. I wouldn't work with a program that doesn't do something," Patton said (Topeka Daily Capital, May, 1967).

Residents were very sensitive to the attentions and shifting perceptions of people outside Highland Park-Pierce. "The city is talking about us out here!" exclaimed a resident who was participating in house activities.

The Chamber of Commerce probably didn't know we even existed before, but now they are interested in what we are doing and want to help us. We are causing some buzzing at City Hall, too. We are showing people that we have got it, and we've got the city's eyes on us.

Another resident added, philosophically, "No, we used to have the city's eyes on us before, but they were looking down at us. Now, we look straight into each other's eyes, man to man, like it oughta be."

The activities and successes of the Highland Park-Pierce Neighborhood House have stimulated the interest of residents and committees in other Topeka OEO target areas. Several Neighborhood Committee officers have attended or held meetings in the Highland Park-Pierce House, and have called upon house staff to work with them on various problems. Following the example of Highland Park-Pierce, and at the same time prodded by an "if they can do it, so can we" sense of competition, six other target neighborhoods have at this writing made application to the regional Office of Economic Opportunity for funds with which to establish their own houses.

Room for Dissent

With longevity, there came to the house a wider variety of resident opinions and attitudes concerning neighborhood activities and social action. "Oldtimers," after a year's contact with the house, tended now to view their social environment with less skepticism and more confidence than residents who might just be beginning to become involved. Furthermore, the opportunity for participant democracy in house and neighborhood committee meetings invited and stimulated debate on issues important to the neighborhood. At times, meetings would become heated as the participants tested their ideas and, most significantly, themselves in a climate where discussion was free and open. In such a climate, emotional as well as intellectual restrictions were lifted, with the result that in some meetings, as a participant remembered, "It was difficult to tell what we did more—cuss or discuss." (For a discussion of the cathartic dynamics of poverty program Neighborhood Action Committee meetings see: Zurcher, 1967c.)

Members differed in the degree to which they were willing to trust representatives of agencies and social organizations. They differed in the degree to which they thought the poor or the Negro could effectively become involved in the "system," without actually having to overthrow that system. They argued not only about specific activities, but the strategy and tactics for implementing the activities. The participants, depending upon the degree and kind of experience they had had with others, varied in their values for future orientation, achievement motivation, activity, and in their willingness to gamble with something new. These differences, and the climate for unhindered expression, generated some volatile discussions, most of which had opportunity to work themselves to a conclusion, and most of which seemed profitable and educational for the participants. "What I like about the meetings," testified a participant, "is that you can say what you want. Oh, people let you have it because they don't agree with you! But you can speak your mind right back at them. Sometimes you're right and sometimes you're wrong, but you're never ashamed."

Several indigenous leaders emerged within the neighborhood house, over the months of its operation. On occasion, indigenous leaders with contrasting approaches or opinions would clash. Cliques would form, do battle, interact, merge, divide, etc. In the neighborhood house no one was obliged to remain affixed permanently to any rigid set of opinions. It now seemed explicitly or implicitly understood by most participants that the purpose of the house was to stimulate social change—and that meant change in opinions, values, and attitudes about self, neighborhood, and community. Consensus and dissension were essential to the process. The internalization of neighborhood and community identity and the evolution of a united approach toward social action did not seem to mean that the participant had to sacrifice his individuality. On the contrary, often his individuality appeared to be enhanced by his increasing ability to operate successfully in widening social spheres.

In May, 1967, the Highland Park-Pierce Neighborhood Committee conducted its annual election, through the neighborhood house. Each of the three offices, chairman, vice-chairman and secretary, was contested by at least two candidates. The election held prior to the existence of the house polled a total of 19 votes from the neighborhood. The 1967 election, held in the house, polled 51 votes. The number still was too small, as far as the house staff were concerned, and in 1968 they planned to "bring the ballot box around to each home in the neighborhood." The number of votes, however, seems less small when it is understood that the total votes cast in the Highland Park-Pierce Neighborhood Committee election surpassed the total number of votes cast for all the officers in all nine other Target Neighborhood Committees combined. Furthermore, Highland Park-Pierce was the only election that had contested ballots for all offices.

At one of their meetings residents talked about the value of conflict. Unanimously they condemned violent conflict. Some members were against violence for practical reasons—"It just doesn't pay off"; "You might end up getting hurt yourself"; "Maybe it is necessary when you have no other course of action to take, but everything else ought to be tried first"; "You may have to do that when you're locked up in a ghetto in a big city, but I don't think we have to do that kind of thing here in Topeka."

Other members were more philosophical about the issue: "It isn't right to get ahead by walking over other people"; "There is something wrong with trying to get dignity for yourself by smashing the dignity of other people."

Nonviolent conflict, however, was almost unanimously endorsed by the residents. To them nonviolent conflict meant the juxtaposing of just with unjust practices, of prejudice with acceptance, of freedom with restriction. It meant, "expressing ourselves out in the open with ideas for change that lots of people may be opposed to"; "making sure you get your say in things, even when there hasn't been any room for your say before"; "getting your opinion out about your rights to those who you know will be opposed."

To the residents discussing the issue, conflict was not an end in itself. "It's no good hitting your head against the wall, just to hit it against the wall." Rather, it was considered to be a strategy for, "getting the issues important to our lives on the community's agenda. It's a way of getting people to look at the problems of poverty, when they don't even think that poverty exists in Topeka."

The residents seem to have established latitude within their own neighborhood house for healthy dissent. Increasingly, they are demonstrating their dissent with societal restrictions that perpetuate the cycle of poverty. But, through the neighborhood house, they have been able to register dissent in a constructive fashion — toward cooperative individual and community social change. In this way they have not had to dissociate themselves from and attack the community, but rather have been able to contribute to it for the benefit of themselves and all its citizens.

Chapter 6

Why Is It Working?

THE Highland Park-Pierce Neighborhood House appears
to be functioning as intended and, at least at this writing,
meeting the expectations of the Economic Opportunity Act.
A number of circumstances, some planned and some accidental,
seem to have contributed to the neighborhood house's progress
thus far—circumstances that may limit or facilitate generalization
of the Highland Park-Pierce case to other locations and populations.

Topeka's poverty conditions, though perhaps similar to those
in rural and other small or middle-sized midwest urban communities, do not compare in magnitude or concentration with poverty
conditions in the nation's large urban centers. Though the individual's experience of poverty and the social processes
sustaining poverty may be similar in both Topeka and larger
cities, Topeka lacks the ghettoization that intensifies and makes
more apparent to public view that experience and those processes. Even in Highland Park-Pierce, Topeka's most poverty-

stricken area, the poor have in the past suffered in quiet and detached silence. The absence of multiple family units and, when compared with tenement settings, the relatively large distance between dwellings seem to help prevent shared expressions of suffering and concerted action toward poverty amelioration. Topeka in the past has manifested no marked militancy among the poor, nor among ethnic minorities in general. Yet despite the lack of group feeling and group action, nonetheless there apparently was much awareness by individuals of their own plight, and of the actions people were taking in other communities toward the resolution of poverty and inequality. The low-income areas of Topeka, and particularly the Highland Park-Pierce Neighborhood, apparently were ripe for such a social intervention innovation as a neighborhood house.

Circumstances Contributing to Progress

The geographical size and population of Highland Park-Pierce may also have made it an ideal setting for a neighborhood house. Twelve hundred people in 400 clearly boundaried acres are compact and manageable, and provide a perceivable "turf" to be served by a neighborhood house.

The founding philosophy and rationale for the Topeka OEO, and the managerial style of its charter staff, encouraged participation of the poor and subsequently provided opportunity for the development of flexible role relationships between OEO and house staffs.

Prior to the opening of the neighborhood house and starting with the funding of the Topeka OEO, Highland Park-Pierce had a viable and active Target Neighborhood Committee, three of whose members had been elected officers. The charismatic characteristics of those three neighborhood officers, their own experiences with poverty, and their familiarity with the area in which they lived, significantly contributed to the evolution toward establishment of a neighborhood house. All three officers were poor, but had some limited leadership experience in lay church activities. None of the officers were looking for a "way out" of Highland Park-Pierce, but declared that they had become involved in the Poverty Program for humanitarian or religious reasons. The indigenous leadership, therefore, intended to remain identified with Highland Park-Pierce and its people. For example, the chairman of the Neighborhood Committee, though he accepted election as chairman of all the Neighborhood Committee officers and as vice-chairman of the Economic Opportunity Board, declined an invitation to apply for a paid job with the Topeka Office of Economic Opportunity. He admitted that he was tempted by the offer, but refused because he felt the job would preclude his "representing the opinions of the people in Highland Park-Pierce." Also, all three neighborhood officers indicated that they felt as many residents as possible should have an opportunity to experience leadership. Following this belief, the officers established numerous committee and subcommittee rotating chairmanships.

Furthermore, the Highland Park-Pierce Neighborhood Committee had, prior to application for the neighborhood house, gained proposal and process experience with the Extension Worker Program. They had felt both enthusiasm and frustration concerning that program, and profited from what they perceived to have been their share of the mistakes contributing to the neighborhood's loss of program control.

The two agencies that contributed money or services to provide a local share for the Federal funding of the neighborhood house also manifested characteristics that provided an optimum climate for house development. The Menninger Foundation, with long experience in the psychiatric arts, was committed to the urgency of developing new techniques for prevention and treatment of mental illness among the poor. The clinical staff of the foundation saw the neighborhood house as a possible prototype for a program of community mental health centers, and as a potential training ground for physicians interested in community psychiatry. At the outset, therefore, the basis for justifying assignment of foundation funds to the neighborhood house was utilitarian—the house might serve as a means for the gathering of data which in turn could be used for mental health applications. The clinical staff gave some early thought to the importance of house autonomy, but by no means concurred on the issue. Very shortly after the neighborhood house began to operate, the clinical staff of the foundation, influenced by their own observations and by reports from the present authors, agreed that freedom for growth toward autonomy was indeed a central dynamic for individual and social change through the neighborhood house. Any plans for establishing therapy or physician training within the house were shelved unless and until the residents of Highland Park-Pierce should themselves ask for them. Perhaps most interesting was the fact that the neighborhood house, even in its early days, influenced the operating policy of its major supporting organization. The Menninger Foundation now justified its commitment by taking the position that the neighborhood house was more than a *means* for gathering data later to be used by mental health practitioners among the poor. Rather, the house was *itself* a potentially effective strategy for mental health. Thus the Highland Park-Pierce Neighborhood House had the advantage of a supporting organization that would provide funding without restrictive expectations, and whose organizational structure and policies were flexible enough to accommodate innovations toward its goals of prevention and cure of mental illness.

The second agency supporting the house with local support, the Cooperative Extension Service, similarly was open to innovation for accomplishing its organizational goals.

The Extension Service had in the past primarily concentrated on bringing technical services to rural areas. Currently, however, it was broadening its scope of work to include urban poor. State and county officials came to the Highland Park Neighborhood Committee, and subsequently to the Highland Park-Pierce

Neighborhood House, with admitted lack of expertise on urban poverty problems. They freely accepted invitations for their technical services in homemaking, property rehabilitation, youth projects, etc., and candidly asked questions of residents concerning how best to work with the poor. Therefore, the Highland Park-Pierce participants in extension programs found themselves in other than a strictly receiving position, and were able to return advice for advice. The Extension Service, since it had no fixed policy for dealing with the urban poor in the Topeka area, was receptive to suggestions and able to improvise programming.

As they continued their working relationship with the neighborhood house, extension agents began to perceive it not only as a source of expertise in itself, but as a partner in the dissemination of technical services and skills to the poor.

Though the client-to-colleague relationship evolved over a period of time, the neighborhood house received from its beginning the unanimous approval of many of the community's agencies and organizations. A primary reason for that acceptance was that those agencies and organizations had representatives on the Economic Opportunity Board who had been meeting together regularly for over a year. The members of the board had to a greater or lesser degree become familiar with and understood the goals of the local poverty program as formulated by the Topeka OEO. The board had considered and unanimously approved the Highland Park-Pierce proposal for a neighborhood house, and thus members were apprised not only of its purposes but its particulars. The agency and organization representatives' involvement with the neighborhood house, even if merely to vote approval, helped to provide a base of community support for the house and facilitated the further development of working relationships.

The neighborhood house was not perceived by citizens in the community-at-large as being a threat. The house's goals for neighborhood and individual improvement, and the increased utilization of services among the poor, harmonized with overall community goals. The leaders of Highland Park-Pierce were from within Topeka, and were not "outsiders." The philosophy of the neighborhood house promulgated principles of self-help and achievement, which were highly valued within the community. The neighborhood house was not perceived to be political or militant, or to be declaring war on the "haves."

A vital resource that contributed to the functioning of the neighborhood house was its leadership. The importance of the charisma, dedication, and neighborhood identification of the Neighborhood Committee officers and the house staff cannot be overemphasized. The commitment of the Advisory Council members and the house social worker was another key factor contributing to the workings of the house. All of those individuals brought to the neighborhood house specific knowledges and skills that they shared with the others. However, perhaps their most important characteristic was their ability to shed temporarily their accustomed social and/or professional roles, adapting particularistically to one another and to the unique task of developing a neighborhood house. The Highland Park-Pierce Neighborhood House was intended to bring about, through innovation, individual and social change. Most likely it could not have begun that task if among its principal participants there had not been individuals who were themselves willing to innovate with their own social roles, and to tolerate resulting ambiguities, uncertainties, and conflicts.

The Highland Park-Pierce Neighborhood House, as indicated above, was touched by a number of circumstances that contributed to the fashion in which it functioned up to this writing. Whether or not the house can continue to operate with purposive autonomy remains to be seen. Will community resistances to and pressures upon the neighborhood house become more severe when and if the house becomes increasingly outspoken on issues of civil rights? At what point would burgeoning action-orientation begin to alienate cooperating agencies and organizations? Will the neighborhood house become increasingly formalized, become more distant from the poor, and suffer the consequences of its own institutionalization?

How the house will accommodate new stresses and strains is a matter for speculation, and some speculations will be made in the conclusion of this monograph. The following example, however, gives an indication of the level of the house's organizational development, and the response of its principals to a perceived threat.

Managerial Succession and a Challenge to Purposive Autonomy

The Highland Park-Pierce Neighborhood House established and works to maintain functional independence of the Topeka Office of Economic Opportunity and agencies contributing local share of funding. The autonomy is not one of rebellion or protest, as sometimes is seen when individuals have no other way to gain a sense of dignity. Rather, the neighborhood house appears to have established a purposive and cooperative autonomy—an autonomy that is consistent with the importance of ownership and consistent with the basic expectations of the Economic Opportunity Act. Rebellious autonomy, usually a last-ditch mechanism, generally is hostile, rigid, predominantly emotional, and can contribute to further alienation. Purposive autonomy is goal-oriented, nondefensive, flexible, predominantly rational, and cooperative (Zurcher, 1967c). Purposive autonomy, as manifested by the Highland Park-Pierce Neighborhood House, does not result in isolation from the community-at-large.

The case history of the house seems to demonstrate that evolution toward self-direction and purposive autonomy can have positive benefits not only for participants, but for neighborhood and community as well. Growth toward purposive autonomy in the Highland Park-Pierce Neighborhood House would have been impossible without the cooperation and understanding of the nonrestricting supporting organizations. Residents of Highland Park-Pierce were able to select their own Advisory Council for the house, choose their contributing agencies, draw up their own budget, hire their house staff from the neighborhood, and accept responsibility for the operation of the house. The Topeka OEO staff, representing the Economic Opportunity Board, struggled to find a balance between their responsibility for overall program administration and the neighborhood house's evolution toward increasing self-responsbility. The Topeka OEO staff had committed themselves to the principles of the Economic Opportunity Act, particularly to the mandate for participation of the poor. Consequently, after some constructive controversy, a working partnership developed between neighborhood house and Topeka OEO—an agreement that the Topeka OEO was to be an important and useful, but junior and nonrestricting, partner. The keynote of the relationship was flexibility. The Topeka OEO staff became, for any given situation, prepared to run the gamut from total noninterference in house activities to major administrative and/or consultative support—at the request of the neighborhood house staff. The house staff realized that the Topeka OEO had to answer to national OEO, and cooperated in record-keeping and procedural responsibilities.

In December, 1966, the original director of the Topeka OEO resigned to take a position on the staff of the newly elected governor of Kansas. The assistant director assumed responsibility for program administration. Two months later, the Economic Opportunity Board, after a personnel search procedure, hired a new director—who subsequently replaced the original OEO staff with a staff of his own.

The roles, rules, and relationships worked out between the neighborhood house and the Topeka OEO by the interaction of their respective staffs were no longer operative. The original staff had been involved in planning the Topeka OEO and implementing that plan. They had become committed to an organizational rationale that included not only involvement of the poor, but flexibility to accommodate individual and social changes that such involvement would engender. Though they were not always able to do so, the original staff attempted to sustain a climate for Topeka's poverty program in which the process experience for the participating poor was held to be at least as important as program content and administrative efficiency.

The new director and his staff, none of whom had been involved in developing the Topeka OEO's *raison d'être,* appeared primarily to be interested in the content rather than process of poverty programs. As he attempted to implement the organizational style he thought best, the new director encountered difficulty with the neighborhood house staff and Advisory Council.

One of the first difficulties centered around the neighborhood house's published statement that a Model Police Project in Topeka would be more appropriate if it were supported by a Model City Project. According to its director, the Topeka OEO had "been accused of taking a controversial stand" on the Police Project, when in fact "that position was taken by the neighborhood house." Furthermore, the Topeka OEO director felt that the neighborhood house publicity was not "promoting the Topeka OEO." Acting upon his convictions, the Topeka OEO director sent the following memorandum to the house:

RE: NEWS RELEASES AND CORRESPONDENCE

Pursuant to "Policies Governing Selection and Appointment," Section II, Article D. Sub-section 1, the following policy shall be incorporated in every employees personnel file.

Any news release, publication, or correspondence which related to the Topeka Office of Economic Opportunity must be cleared at least one (1) day in advance of issuance by the Director of the Program.

The term "cleared" will be defined as "presented to the director in writing prior to publication." This applies to personal correspondence on OEO letterheads as well as neighborhood newsletters.

The neighborhood house staff, Advisory Council, and many residents considered this action to be censorship and an attack upon their integrity as a responsible neighborhood and community group.

Further following his preferred managerial style, the Topeka OEO director began gathering services-in-kind and preparing the budget for the neighborhood house's refunding by regional OEO. In addition, he hired and assigned a neighborhood coordinator who, directly under his supervision, would be responsible for all neighborhood activities. These actions and decisions were interpreted by neighborhood house staff, Advisory Council, and many residents to have been done without their involvement, and thus to be a restriction of their freedom and a repudiation of their demonstrated responsibility and integrity. "We've come a long way since the house first began," exclaimed an angry resident, "and now it looks like we're supposed to go back into the cradle again!"

On September 7, 1967, the Neighborhood House Advisory Council met, responding to their perception that the "philosophy of the neighborhood house" was being threatened. They decided to invite the Topeka OEO director to meet with them and discuss "how he saw the relationship with the Administrative Office and the neighborhood house." Further they wished to discuss the prerogatives of budget preparation, services-in-kind, and publicity. The Topeka OEO director met with the Advisory Council as invited, and a heated discussion resulted. Subsequently, the director and council have met again, and have also exchanged a number of written communications.

From the encounters, it seems clear that the house staff and participants, having evolved purposive autonomy and personal dignity through their house, would not be willing or able to retreat from what they refer to as "the mainstream of the community." It also seems clear, at this time, that the new staff of the Topeka OEO have not yet found for themselves a workable balance between administrative control and maximum feasible participation of the poor, between program content and beneficiary process experience. However, both house and Topeka OEO staff are continuing to maintain opportunities for direct confrontation with the issues and with each other; thus there remains opportunity for workable role boundaries and functional relationships to emerge.

The experience with Topeka OEO managerial succession, some fears about the future of national OEO, indices of community-based support, and urgings from the Advisory Council and residents have prompted the neighborhood house staff to formally file articles of incorporation with the state of Kansas. Incorporation of the house seems further to manifest the intensity of resident sense of ownership, and enacts the national OEO expectation that local resources increasingly provide backing for poverty programs initially predominantly funded by the Federal government. As a corporation, the house will have more diverse access to funding. Thus neighborhood residents will be able to consider a broader range of alternatives for need satisfaction, and consequently the house will have increased versatility for negotiation and for innovation programming.

Chapter 7

Concluding Statements

Neighborhood House versus Neighborhood Facility

TO establish conceptual contrast and stimulate further discussion, we shall arbitrarily distinguish between a "neighborhood house" and a "neighborhood facility." By neighborhood facility we mean an outpost of an already established community organization or agency, which has been physically placed in a low-income neighborhood without the active participation of residents in its planning, implementation, and operation. The primary goal of a neighborhood facility is to extend the outreach of the parent organization to a wider audience. Direction and programming for the facility are provided from outside the neighborhood in accordance with the parent organization's superordinate goals. Staffing of the facility may include employees from both inside and outside the neighborhood, but hiring is done by the parent organization, following their own personnel policies and procedures. The neighborhood facility is program-oriented, the beneficiaries are considered to be clients, and its function is to service residents of the neighborhood. The facility's ability systematically to communicate or get information to residents is far more sophisticated than its ability systematically to communicate with or gain information from the residents. The expectation of the parent organization that operations immediately be efficient is more important to the neighborhood facility than procedural innovations that may temporarily be inefficient. Indigenous nonprofessionals who work for the facility are considered to be agency employees, and are expected to internalize an agency identity. The parent organization sees the neighborhood facility to be completely and directly under its jurisdiction and administrative control. Involvement in social action is eschewed, particularly if controversial issues are at stake. The parent organization disassociates itself from any conflict that might impair its image or put it at odds with representatives from other agencies, service organizations or local government. The neighborhood facility reflects the same cautiousness and conservativeness.

The neighborhood facility may, in fact, be quite efficient in promulgating and effecting its services throughout a neighborhood. Residents may indeed appreciate and avail themselves of those services. However, residents do not experience a sense of ownership or participation in the facility's operation, Furthermore, a significant number of them may perceive the facility with stereotyped suspicion and distrust, writing it off as "another one of those agencies that tells us what to do and where to go, without ever really helping us to change anything."

The functions, goals and general operation of a neighborhood house, as indicated in the case history presented thus far, stand in contrast to those of a neighborhood facility as we have defined it. From its outset, the neighborhood house is concerned with the participation of residents in planning, implementing, and operating not only the house itself, but all programs based in the house. Directions and administration of the house are from inside, rather than outside the neighborhood; staff are hired from among residents by residents. The house may depend upon an organization or organizations for funding, but the support is essentially non restrictive. Contributing and/or cooperating organizations see the neighborhood house as a means of extending their services but, importantly, at the invitation of the residents. Furthermore, those organizations clearly understand and accept that the neighborhood house is intended to stimulate growth and therefore change within the neighborhood and among its residents. The house is expected to accommodate the growth it stimulates, and therefore cannot be burdened with inflexible superordinate organization policies. The organizations appreciate the potential of a relatively autonomous neighborhood house not only as a way further to increase service outreach, but as an innovative strategy toward amelioration of social problems.

The neighborhood house is person-oriented rather than program-oriented, although the importance of worthwhile and desired programs is not underestimated. The people who come into contact with the house are not clients, but neighbors and partners. Communication is not felt to exist unless it is two-way; information without dialogue increases the individual's knowledge, but does not disrupt entrenched passivity broadly enough. The neighborhood house is concerned with the efficiency of its programs, but quest for efficiency is not considered to be more important than the participation of the residents in program determination. Though resident participation may at times temporarily impede bureaucratic efficiency, it is taken to be the most efficient means available to promulgate self-esteem among the participating poor. Indigenous nonprofessionals work for the people of the neighborhood, and not for an abstract and distant agency.

Perhaps the most important difference between a neighborhood facility and a neighborhood house is that the latter affords residents the opportunity to evolve an organization, for which they feel ownership, at their pace and by their own direction. That evolution can include individual change stimulated by participation, gradual socialization into new roles, the acquisition of more adaptive skills, and a shifting view of neighborhood and community. An initial emphasis upon short-term goals for the house

—manifested by residents' calls for quick attention to individual problems and for immediately accomplishable projects—may develop, as skills and competencies increase, into longer range neighborhood and community concerns. The opportunity provided by the house for successful encounters with previously frightening community power components often accomplishes significant personal change among residents: trust may replace suspicion; activity may replace passivity; achievement may replace failure; self-confidence may replace feelings of inferiority; a sense of worth may replace a sense of worthlessness; commitment may replace withdrawal. As a neighborhood house operates over time, it can accumulate a history that is shared by residents. The experience of self-determined history-making, plus increasing confidence that things can be changed, can yield increased future orientation. Involvement of residents through the neighborhood house, and meaningful social action that expands to include not only neighborhood but the community-at-large, can break down feelings of isolation, powerlessness, normlessness, and other components of general alienation. One observer, describing the impact of a neighborhood house, reports:

> Besides the physical accomplishments of the Neighborhood organizations, other changes have taken place which are worthy of note. In the Neighborhood House area one is aware of a marked alteration in the attitude of the residents. Apathy and defeatism have been replaced by interest and optimism. People seem closer to each other, now that they plan and work together for the future. The Neighborhood radiates a feeling of cohesiveness . . .In the case of this Neighborhood a climate needed to be developed so that people could relate to one another in an atmosphere of trust and confidence. . .Once established, the climate enabled the individual members involved to be recognized as individuals. . .The process involved in the attempt to improve one's Neighborhood increases knowledge. . .becomes a learning experience. . .In a world of large institutional and corporate control, it becomes increasingly vital for the individual to know that he has some influence on his own future. . .The Neighborhood worker also tends to have personal involvement in the plans for successful implementation, a factor too often overlooked by local, state and Federal agencies and professionals engaged in urban programs. . .A further motivational factor which seems to influence the behavior of the citizens around the Neighborhood House should

be mentioned. It is imperative to people that their life be of some worth, their actions worthwhile. This need is difficult to meet in everyday occupations of the city dwellers, but working with fellow citizens for the betterment of one's Neighborhood is one way. Each person achieves a satisfying sense that he is serving the society in which he lives (Criminger, 1966, pp. 101-104).

Brager (1965), Fishman and Solomon (1963), Leighton (1965), Perlman and Jones (1967), Piven (1966), Riessman (1965a, 1965b), Riessman and Hallowitz (1967), and Wittenberg (1948) further discuss the impact upon the poor of their participation in meaningful, self-determined social action.

The neighborhood house can become an instrument for social change; efforts toward change, as well as accomplished change, are expected to engender conflict. The neighborhood house and its supporting organizations understand the social benefits of nonviolent conflict. As a result, residents have the opportunity to experience conflict without hatred — purposeful conflict associated with social change, which reshapes roles and expectations and modifies social structure without being destructive to other human beings.

Over time, the neighborhood house has the potential to become more concerned with integrating the neighborhood and stimulating resident cohesion than in servicing the residents — though the importance of services and agency expertise are not overlooked. Since there is more concern with social change through concerted action, the neighborhood house almost inevitably will be more controversial than the neighborhood facility.

From a psychological point of view, the heart of the Economic Opportunity Act is the mandate that the poor shall be colleagues in and not just clients of the program. The hypothesis is that the process experience of meaningful participation will enhance self-worth and help to break the entrapping cycle of poverty. Though still young and growing, the Highland Park-Pierce Neighborhood House seems already to be evidence that this hypothesis, when given a chance to work in a climate of freedom and acceptance, can be accurate.

A crucial dynamic of the neighborhood house is the sense of ownership experienced by people who live in the area. This sense of ownership contributes to individual and neighborhood identity and pride. Ownership also brings with it the burden of decision-making and responsibility — burdens welcomed, because they are part of the price of dignity and respect that the poor are seldom given the opportunity to pay.

Though important, a building and available services do not make a neighborhood house. The total dynamic of a neighborhood house, such as the one in Highland Park-Pierce, cannot be prefabricated and dropped into X area. Rather, the house slowly evolves with the development of trust and confidence in both the staff, who should come from the neighborhood itself, and in the idea. Skepticism, suspicion, disbelief that this really is "our" and not "their" house erodes as participants discover there are no contracts demanded, legal or psychological. The only rank in this group is neighbor, the only relevant authority is we. From this experience of identity can grow not only self-realization, but awareness of neighborhood and community. Feelings of trust, responsibility, potency and dignity generated by participation in the neighborhood house can generalize to the individual's activities in the wider community — particularly when the house, as has Highland Park-Pierce, interacts with other community agencies and local government for the improvement of their neighborhood. The alienated have the opportunity realistically to assess what parts of their alienation can be attributed to defensive self-exile, lack of skills, or changeable social conditions, and what can be done about the debilitating factors.

Numerous community agencies cooperate with and make services available through the neighborhood house. An important difference is that the house provides a bridge between community agencies and the poor, and provides an all-important personal touch in situations where the agency workload or organization leaves little time for individual consideration. Also, another important difference is that the participants can perceive the agencies to be involved at the request of their house. The participants thus may view the agencies as useable and service oriented, and not, according to the stereotype, as monolithic and exploitative. The participants can begin to feel, as do their financially better-off counterparts, some control in interactions with large organizations, and subsequently in the community-at-large.

Some Suggestions for Further Research

Neighborhood organizations intended to stimulate social change can provide ideal settings for studies of adult socialization, the relationship of individual to social processes, and the interaction of personality and organization. This report of individual and social consequences of a neighborhood house is based upon a single case. Though the Highland Park-Pierce House was rather extensively studied by participant observation, unstructured interview and record examination, the research nonetheless must be considered exploratory. Generalizations to include neighborhood houses serving varying populations in other geographical locations must be made cautiously.

Structured interviews and mechanical recording devices, where and when appropriate, could effectively be used in tandem with participant observation, data from the former strengthening the reliability of data from the latter. The present study primarily focused upon those individuals who were active participants in the neighborhood house — i.e., staff, committee members, Advisory Council members, those who were involved in various classes, subcommittees, programs, activities, etc. Secondarily, the study focused upon those individuals who were not active in but had been directly served by the house. No data were gathered and consequently no comments made about residents who were neither active in nor directly served by the house. Further research might profitably employ survey techniques with a random and representative sample of neighborhood residents, thus yielding comparisons of participants with non-participants and generating broader indices of neighborhood house effectiveness for individual and social change.

Studying and comparing neighborhood houses more systematically and over a longer period of time would provide an opportunity for the investigator to make more certain statements about the impact of those houses as social innovators. It should be remarked, however, that research for a specific neighborhood house, or for any social intervention organization, must be tailored to and not interfere with its strategies and goals. The research should not itself be a resistance to social change.

Some Suggestions for Practitioners

Despite acknowledged limitations of interpretations based upon an exploratory study of a single case, we speculate and present, at least for discussion, the following suggestions to those who would implement a neighborhood house. Though the suggestions will be arbitrarily stated, each should be considered as much hypothesis as recommendation:

1. The *neighborhood house* beginning with a service orientation that encourages beneficiaries to initiate contacts with agencies and organizations can be expected to evolve an action-orientation. Increasing successful and self-determined experiences with agencies and organizations tend to encourage a sense of personal efficacy within the environment, and to stimulate individual confidence for attempts toward environmental change. Residents who have shared the modified relationship with complex organizations are likely to form groups for ad hoc neighborhood action, often for improvement or beautification of physical surroundings. That rudimentary action, if successful, probably will lead to wider resident participation in activities for social change that involve not only the neighborhood but the community-at-large.

The neighborhood house should not be considered a preformed organization placed full-blown in a neighborhood, all of whose residents expect or even want the house. More likely, particularly in disorganized neighborhoods where the only sense of cohesion results from geographical or social boundaries, the initial impetus for the house will stem from the interest of a relatively small cohort of residents. Through the work of that cohort, increasing numbers of residents will become involved, and the house will function to help create a resident-validated sense of neighborhood. Paralleling the burgeoning neighborhood identity will be the gradual expansion of the house's initial orientation for services to include orientation for social action. The neighborhood house, therefore, should in no fashion be conceptualized as a static organization. Rather, its central dynamic is the evolution of structure and function to accommodate resident needs and changes.

2. The organizational style, policies, and practices of the OEO *community action agency* (CAA) can significantly determine the effectiveness of a neighborhood house as an innovating social intervener. The rationale of the CAA should be broad enough and its management flexible enough to permit the growth of a neighborhood house toward cooperative and purposive autonomy. The CAA staff, whose basic commitment should be to the poor and the community rather than to the source of funding, ideally would not define organizational integrity to include the necessity for rigid control and centralization. Rather, they would view the neighborhood house as potentially evolving into an important confederate in the community's overall war on poverty. The CAA should not impede the house's evolution toward purposive autonomy by managerial arbitrariness. The CAA staff should, for example, interpret directives and memoranda from national OEO as much as possible to maximize freedom of direction and choice of alternatives by resident participants. On the other hand, the CAA staff should not equate the stimulation of purposive autonomy with total abandonment of the house. The neighborhood house staff will need the accumulated expertise of the CAA staff, and such expertise will

be particularly useful if acquired by invitation. Total abandoning of the neighborhood house to "go it alone" may make the house's task considerably more difficult, or in fact condemn the house to failure. Such a lack of support may be a not too subtle means of organizational control, saying in effect "stay under our direction or you'll see what will happen." The outcome could be a self-fulfilling prophecy concerning the potential for individual and social change among the poor through the growth of purposive autonomy in a neighborhood house—"you see, we give them a chance to make it on their own, and they fall apart!" The CAA should be prepared to support the neighborhood house with such technical and moral support as it requests, and the CAA staff should remember that those requests may not follow a predictable pattern.

The CAA should expect individual and social change to be the result of a successful neighborhood house. That means more than giving lip service to the possibility for such changes, but a willingness to accommodate the consequences of growth toward autonomy including the evolution of a new set of role relationships among the participants. Furthermore, the CAA should clearly understand the differences between, but equal importance of, the content of specific programs and the process experience of participation in formulating and implementing the programs. Every effort should be made to provide meaningful alternatives for choices of program content, and to maintain open opportunity for meaningful process experience.

The CAA should anticipate conflicts and expectations between neighborhood residents and the participating not-poor, and should be prepared to mediate those conflicts toward mutual understanding. The differences in expectations among participants, including the CAA staff, should be considered part of the agenda of social change, and should be verbalized, discussed and reevaluated as they evolve, in open discussion among all the participants. Consequently, training programs provided for the participants by the CAA staff should include not only a wide range of materials concerning program content, but should also include and emphasize continuing assessments of the dynamics of the process experience and social change.

The community action agency should prepare as much as possible a base of community support for beginning neighborhood houses, and sustain that support throughout the evolution of the house. The latter would be particularly crucial when a neighborhood house, as it stimulates social change, becomes involved in controversy. The CAA staff should themselves understand and should promulgate understanding that controversy and role conflict are a natural result of change, and can result in a constructive breaking down of individual and group rigidities, especially when the opportunity for free, open, and equal status communication among all participants is maintained. The maintenance of that communication is the responsibility of the CAA itself. The CAA should try to maintain within its own organization and among others involved a model of participant democracy that includes both consensus and dissent, a model that may be emulated by the neighborhood house.

The CAA should not evaluate a neighborhood house solely in terms of bureaucratic or "hard" efficiency. The number of contacts, followups, service rendered, etc., may be important criteria of house accomplishment. However, the more difficult to measure "soft" operations of the house—those more specifically concerned with individual and the group change—are at a minimum equally important. Those can be measured at least indirectly: by the increasing involvement of residents in neighborhood and community affairs; by subjective reports of increased self-confidence and pride, and of enhanced self-image; and by the willingness of residents to gamble with new and more active social roles. Also, the numbers of participants may at first be discouragingly small, particularly in those areas where little sense of neighborhood existed prior to the establishment of the house. Such numbers should be judged relatively and not absolutely. If 30 individuals are participating in a program toward neighborhood improvement where previously there were no participants, then involvement should be considered to have increased thirtyfold, and those 30 considered to be the vanguard of more to follow. Furthermore, if several of the early participants seem to be previously experienced indigenous leaders in the neighborhood, the program should not be despaired of for not yet having reached the inexperienced. It should be understood that indigenous leadership, having the opportunity to exert itself in new roles and under less restrictive social conditions, may be the most efficient way to reach greater numbers of inexperienced or alienated residents. If the neighborhood house first has to create a sense of neighborhood among residents, then one cannot expect at the onset mass neighborhood response.

The CAA may, over time, become increasingly formalized and institutionalized. If that is the case, the CAA should strive to maintain neighborhood houses that can remain relatively informal and noninstitutional, thus sustaining conditions that maximize possibilities for reaching the poor in an innovative fashion.

The most important criterion for selecting a structure in which to base a neighborhood house is resident preference. The CAA should not be more concerned with the physical "image" of the building than with its potential to stimulate a sense of ownership, informality, and interpersonal closeness among the participants.

Though the size of the population to be served by a house must be judged on the basis of neighborhood and resident characteristics, the crucial variables are the opportunity for house staff to maintain personal contact with residents, and the ease with which residents can identify with the house and consequently with the neighborhood.

3. Those *community agencies or organizations* who choose to fund a neighborhood house should avoid imposing policy and program restrictions that would interfere with growth toward purposive autonomy or with latitude for social innovation. Ideally, the agencies or organizations would view the neighbor

hood house as a new strategy for accomplishing their more abstract organizational goals, i.e., mental health, amelioration of social problems, etc., and therefore would provide the house with relative freedom from traditional standard operating procedures. Paralleling the relationship between an institutionalized community action agency and the neighborhood house, supporting agencies or organizations might conceptualize the neighborhood house as a comparatively informal and more adaptable organizational form, worthy of support and capable of sharing a social problem work load.

The agencies or organizations realize that the neighborhood house needs both financial and technical backing, but that such backing should be provided at the invitation of residents to whom the neighborhood house will belong.

Those agencies or organizations that would not be able to accept controversy possibly associated with the house's evolution toward purposive autonomy should not attempt to fund the neighborhood house, but at most cooperate only from a distance. Supporting agencies or organizations must be committed to the processes of participative democracy in the neighborhood house, and be willing to gamble upon the consequences.

Those community agencies and organizations who choose to cooperate with or utilize the services of the neighborhood house should view it as a means of extending their outreach, but avoid trying to shape the house in their own image. The agencies or organizations should allow opportunity for residents to shift their conception of community services from professional initiator to beneficiary initiator, and the house staff to modify their roles from clients to colleagues.

4. The neighborhood house and its supporting agencies or organizations may agree to the usefulness of having a professional *participating consultant*. The participating consultant may be a social worker, a psychologist, a psychiatrist, etc. His task is particularly crucial to the success of the neighborhood house, since he is not only an on-the-scene source of technical informa-

tion, but more importantly is a role model undergoing constant appraisal and reappraisal.

His commitment to neighborhood residents and to the principles of the neighborhood house must be obvious; yet he must not be perceived to be alienated from or disenchanted with useful components of the community-at-large. He cannot deny that he is a professional, cannot proclaim that he is "poor," and must not allow himself to romanticize the conditions of poverty. Yet he must be aware of the fact that his effectiveness in the neighborhood house will come not at first from resident value of his professionalism, but rather from his being accepted as a person who can be trusted. While his title may give him immediate acceptance among members of the middle socioeconomic class, that same title may being him suspicion and stereotypy from among the poor. As he becomes accepted as a person, as he establishes equal status interaction with resident participants in the house, as he demonstrates his willingness to learn as well as teach, and as he demonstrates that his knowledge has value simply because it is *useful,* he becomes an effective participating consultant. The consulting contract grows out of the interactive process among the participants, it is not *a priori* in the minds of the consultees.

In the beginning phases of the house's development, the staff and residents may try to orient to the participating consultant as a formal leader. He should make every effort to stay removed from supervisory status and administrative decision-making. He may indeed be a resource person, a provider of alternatives, but should do his best to avoid being part of actual program determinations. He must not allow trust in him to be warped into dependence upon him. Rather, he should allow himself to be trusted and used, and encourage generalizing of that trust and that usability to the organization he represents, and to other similar agencies and organizations.

He will often be called upon by house staff for evaluative opinions. That evaluation should as much as possible be reflective, maximizing the possibility for the staff themselves to work through the appropriateness of their own courses of action. He must provide noncompetitive counsel, and be an individual who is not concerned with establishing a power position for himself within the house.

The participating consultant should discuss continually with neighborhood house staff the content-process duality in poverty intervention, and the kinds of responses such intervention might be expected to elicit from neighborhood participants.

The participating consultant must be comfortable enough with himself to be able to shed professional distance from those with whom he works, and be capable of tolerating initial suspiciousness and rejection from some of the residents. Furthermore, he must be able to accommodate to a marginal position between the supporting organization and the neighborhood house, particularly during those times when he may seem to be receiving positive reinforcement from neither.

5. The *neighborhood house staff* should be indigenous, indigenously chosen. All staff members should be residents of the neighborhood in which the house is to be established, and should manifest a firm commitment to the people of that neighborhood. That commitment may be expressed in humanitarian or religious terms, may reflect an ambition for self or status improvement, but it holds the job to be something more than "a way out" of the neighborhood. All staff members should be person-oriented, empathetic, and able to relate to residents in an informal, nonthreatening fashion.

Most important, all staff members, particularly the director, should have the ability for or the capacity to learn role adaptability in varying social situations with differing components of the community. Consequently, staff members must also have a tolerance for the marginality and role confusion that may result from growth toward that adaptability.

The staff must be able to operate in such a way as to reach both the content and process goals of the poverty program, and to understand and make useful for social change those conflicts that may result in attempts to reach the goals.

The staff, in order to encourage the development of purposive autonomy in the house through resident participation, must be flexible enough in their own staff roles to provide the emergence of additional indigenous leadership, even if emerging leaders begin to challenge or test staff authority.

All staff members should have the opportunity for and be able to respond to continuing training programs on program content and alternatives. Furthermore, staff should be able to invite participant consultants with whom they can reflect upon and express reactions to their own part in the process of social change.

6. The middle socioeconomic class membership of house *advisory councils* may at the onset, advertently or inadvertently, dominate council meetings, thus not giving low-income representation adequate chance to participate fully. The middle-class members will be more practiced and experienced in the techniques and purposes of meetings, and the poor's early silence may be interpreted as a request that middle-class members take charge.

In the neighborhood house advisory council it is not the function of the middle-class members to lead, but to provide strong support to the residents when such support is requested, and to share their knowledges and abilities when invited to do so.

Like the participating consultant, each middle-class member of the advisory council will inevitably be a role model, with potentially positive or negative effects upon the attitudes and behavior of the participating poor. In a very real sense, the middle-class members can be gatekeepers whose example heightens for the poor the desirability or undesirability of social change, and of alternative strategies toward social change.

If a neighborhood house is to follow the mandate of the Economic Opportunity Act and to generate significant individual and social change in a low-income neighborhood, it should provide residents with an opportunity to experience active participation. Active participation includes opportunity to develop a sense of ownership, direction, and control of the neighborhood house and responsibility for its associated programs. Resident identification with the house is thus facilitated and can lead to identification with the neighborhood and the community-at-large. Similarly, resident pride in the house and its activities can enhance pride in self and property, can generalize to pride in both neighborhood and community, and can encourage confidence for sustained purposive autonomy.

The experience of ownership and participation in a neighborhood house makes it possible for individuals previously entrapped in dependency and poverty to acquire, at their own direction and pace, a sense of dignity — and, as reflected by a participant in the Highland Park-Pierce Neighborhood House, "Dignity is what it's all about!"

References

Beilin, H. The pattern of postponability and its relation to social class mobility. *Journal of Social Psychology,* 1956, *44,* 33-48.

Beiser, M. Poverty, social disintegration and personality. In B. H. Kaplan (Ed.), Poverty dynamics and interventions, *Journal of Social Issues,* 1965, *21,* 56-78.

Bell, W. Anomie, social isolation and class structure. *Sociometry,* 1957, *20,* 105-116.

Bernstein, B. Language and social class. *British Journal of Psychology,* 1960, *11,* 271-276.

Brager, G. Organizing the unaffiliated in a low income area. In L. A. Ferman, Joyce L. Kornbluh, & A. Haber (Eds.), *Poverty in America.* Ann Arbor: University of Michigan Press, 1965. Pp. 390-395.

Cohen, A., & Hodges, H. Characteristics of the lower blue collar class. *Social Problems,* 1963, *10,* 303-334.

Cohen, J. Social work and the culture of poverty. *Social Work,* 1964, *9,* 3-10.

Criminger, G. A neighborhood house leads the way. In R. Franklin (Ed.), *Patterns of community development,* Washington, D. C.: Public Affairs Office Press, 1966. Pp. 97-104.

Deutsch, M. P. The disadvantaged child and the learning process. In A. H. Passow (Ed.), *Education in depressed areas.* New York: Columbia University, 1963. Pp. 163-179.

Economic Opportunity Act of 1964, 78, Stat. 508, Title II, Section 202 (A).

Empey, L. J. Social class and occupational aspirations: a comparison of absolute and relative measurements. *American Sociological Review,* 1956, *21,* 703-709.

Fishman, J. R., & Solomon F. Youth and social action: perspectives on the student sit-in movement. *American Journal of Orthopsychiatry,* 1963, *33,* 872-882.

Gans, H. J. Subcultures and class. In L. A. Ferman, Joyce L. Kornbluh, & A. Haber (Eds.), *Poverty in America.* Ann Arbor: University of Michigan Press, 1965. Pp. 302-311.

Gans, H. J. Redefining the settlement's function for the war on poverty. *Social Work,* 1964, *9,* 3-12.

Gould, Rosalind. Some sociological determinants of goal striving. *Journal of Social Psychology,* 1941, *13,* 461-473.

Grosser, C. Local residents as mediators between middle class professional workers and lower class clients. *Social Service Review,* 1966, *XL,* 52-62.

Haggstrom, W. C. The power of the poor. In F. Riessman, J. Cohen, & A. Pearl. (Eds.), *Mental health of the poor.* Glencoe, Ill.: Free Press, 1964, Pp. 205-223.

Harrington, M. *The other America: poverty in the United States.* New York: MacMillan, 1963.

Herzog, Elizabeth. Is there a culture of poverty? In Hannah Meissner (Ed.), *Poverty in the affluent society.* New York: Harper, 1966. Pp. 92-102.

Herzog, Elizabeth. Some assumptions about the poor. *Social Service Review,* 1963, *37,* 391-400.

Keller, Suzanne. The social world of the urban slum child: some early findings. *American Journal of Orthopsychiatry,* 1963, 33, 823-831.

Leighton, A. H. Poverty and social change. *Scientific American,* 1965, *212,* 21-27.

LeShan, L. Time orientation and social class. *Journal of Abnormal and Social Psychology,* 1952, *47,* 589-592.

Levinson, P. Chronic dependency: a conceptual analysis. Social Service Review, 1964, *38,* 371-381.

Lewis, H. Child rearing among low-income families. In L. A. Ferman, Joyce L. Kornbluh, & A. Haber (Eds.), *Poverty in America.* Ann Arbor: University of Michigan Press, 1965. Pp. 342-353.

Lewis, O. *Five families.* New York: Basic Books, 1959.

Lewis, O. *The children of Sanchez.* New York: Random House, 1961.

Lewis, O. *La Vida.* New York: Random House, 1966.

Maccoby, Eleanor. Community integration and the social control of delinquency. *Journal of Social Issues,* 1958, *14,* 38-51.

MacDonald, D. Our invisible poor. In L. A. Ferman, Joyce L. Kornbluh, & A. Haber (Eds.), *Poverty in America.* Ann Arbor: University of Michigan Press, 1965. Pp. 6-24.

McClosky, H., & Schaar, J. H. Psychological dimensions of anomie. *American Sociological Review,* 1965, 30, 14-40.

Miller, S. M. The American lower classes: a typological approach. In A. B. Shostak, & W. Gomberg (Eds.), *New perspective on poverty.* New Jersey: Prentice-Hall, 1966. Pp. 22-40.

Miller, S. M., & Riessman, F. The working class subculture: a new view. *Social Problems,* 1961, *9,* 86-97.

Miller, S. M., Riessman, F., & Seagull, A. Poverty and self-indulgence: a critique of the non-deferred gratification pattern. In L. A. Ferman, Joyce L. Kornbluh, & A. Haber (Eds.), *Poverty in America.* Ann Arbor: University of Michigan Press, 1965. Pp. 285-302.

Miller, W. B. Lower class culture as a generating milieu of gang delinquency. *Journal of Social Issues*, 1958, *14*, 5-19.

Miller, W. B. Focal concerns of lower class culture. In L. A. Ferman, Joyce L. Kornbluh, & A. Haber (Eds.), *Poverty in America*. Ann Arbor: University of Michigan Press, 1965. Pp. 261-270.

Mischel, W. Preference for delayed reinforcement and social responsibility. *Journal of Abnormal and Social Psychology*, 1961, *62*, 1-7.

Ornati, O. Poverty in America. In L. A. Ferman, Joyce L. Kornbluh, & A. Haber (Eds.), *Poverty in America*. Ann Arbor: University of Michigan Press, 1965. Pp. 24-42.

Orshansky, Mollie. Counting the poor: another look at the poverty profile. In L. A. Ferman, Joyce L. Kornbluh, & A. Haber (Eds.), *Poverty in America*. Ann Arbor: University of Michigan Press, 1965. Pp. 42-82.

Pearlman, Helen. Self-determination: reality or illusion? *Social Service Review*, 1965, *39*, 410-422.

Pearlman, R., & Jones, D. *Neighborhood service centers*. Washington, D. C.: U. S. Department of Health, Education, and Welfare, 1967. Pp. 59-60.

Piven, Frances. Participation of residents in neighborhood community action programs. *Social Work*, 1966, *11*, 73-80.

Reiff, R., & Riessman, F. The indigenous nonprofessional: a strategy of change in community action and community health programs. *Community Mental Health Journal* Monograph 1. New York: Behavioral Publications, Inc., 1965.

Riessman, F. Are the deprived nonverbal? In F. Riessman, J. Cohen, & A. Pearl (Eds.), *Mental health of the poor*. Glencoe, Ill.: Free Press, 1964. Pp. 172-187.

Riessman, F. New approaches to mental health treatment of low-income people. In *Social work practice, 1965*. New York: Columbia University Press, 1965. Pp. 174-187. (a)

Riessman, F. New possibilities: services, representation, and careers. Paper read at the planning session for the White House Conference "to fulfill these rights." Washington, D. C., November, 1965. (b)

Riessman, F. *The culturally deprived child*. New York: Harper, 1962.

Riessman, F. The strengths of the poor. In A. B. Shostak, & W. Gomberg (Eds.), *New perspectives on poverty*. New Jersey: Prentice-Hall, 1966. Pp. 40-47.

Riessman, F., Cohen, J., & Pearl, A. *Mental health of the poor*. New York: Free Press, 1964.

Riessman, F., & Hallowitz, E. The neighborhood service center: an innovation in preventive psychiatry. *American Journal of Psychiatry*, 1967, *123*, 1408-1413.

Rodman, H. The lower class value stretch. In L. A. Ferman, Joyce L. Kornbluh,

& A. Haber (Eds.), *Poverty in America*. Ann Arbor: University of Michigan Press, 1965. Pp. 270-284.

Rosen, B. C. The achievement syndrome: a psychocultural dimension of social stratification. *American Sociological Review*, 1956, *21*, 203-211.

Rosen, B. C., & D'Andrade, A. R. Psycho-social origins of achievement motivation. *Sociometry*, 1959, *22*, 185-218.

Schneider, L., & Lysgaard, S. The deferred gratification pattern: a preliminary study. *American Sociological Review*, 1953, *18*, 142-149.

Simpson, R. L., & Miller, M. Social status and alienation. Paper read at Southern Sociological Society, Miami Beach, 1961.

Simpson, R. L., & Miller, M. Social status and anomie. *Social Problems*, 1963, *10*, 256-264.

Sjoberg, G., Brymer, R. A., & Farris B. Bureaucracy and the lower class. *Sociology and Social Research*, 1966, *50*, 325-337.

Spinley, E. M. *The deprived and the privileged*. London: Routledge and Kegan Paul, 1953.

Stone, I. T., Leighton, Dorothea C., & Leighton, A. H. Poverty and the individual. In L. Fishman (Ed.), *Poverty amid affluence*. New Haven: Yale University Press, 1966. Pp. 72-97.

Strauss, M. Deferred gratification, social class, and the achievement syndrome. *American Sociological Review*, 1962, *27*, 326-335.

Topeka OEO Annual Report for 1965-66. Topeka: Topeka Office of Economic Opportunity, 1966. Mimeographed.

Wittenberg, R. M. Personality adjustment through social action. *American Journal of Orthopsychiatry*, 1948, *18*, 207-221.

Wright, C. R., & Hyman, H. H. Voluntary association memberships of American adults: evidence from national sample surveys. *American Sociological Review*, 1958, *23*, 284-294.

Zurcher, L. A. Walking the tight rope: some role and value conflicts experienced by poverty program indigenous leaders. Paper read at American Sociological Association, Miami Beach, August, 1966.

Zurcher, L. A. Functional marginality: dynamics of a poverty intervention organization. *Southwestern Social Science Quarterly*, 1967, *48*, 56-68. (a)

Zurcher, L. A. The leader and the lost: a case study of indigenous leadership in a poverty program community action committee. *Genetic Psychology Monographs*, 1967, *76*, 23-93. (b)

Zurcher, L. A. Stages of development in poverty program neighborhood action committees. *Journal of Applied Behavioral Science*, 1967, *3*. (c)

Zurcher, L. A., & Key, W. H. The overlap model: a comparison of strategies for social change. *Sociological Quarterly*, 1967, *9*, 23-36.